Declarations
of
Dependency

Declarations of Dependency

*The Civic Republican Tradition
in U.S. Poverty Policy*

Alan F. Zundel

State University of New York Press

#4356157

Parts of this work were originally published in *Policy Studies Journal* and are used with their permission: Alan Zundel, "Policy Frames and Ethical Traditions: The Case of Homeownership for the Poor," *PSJ*, 23, 3 (1995): 423–434.

Published by
State University of New York Press, Albany

© 2000 State University of New York

For information, address State University of New York Press,
90 State Street, Suite 700, Albany, N.Y. 12207

Production by Michael Haggett
Marketing by Patrick Durocher

Library of Congress Cataloging-in-Publication Data

Zundel, Alan F., 1952–
   Declarations of dependency : the civic republican tradition in U.S. poverty policy / Alan F. Zundel.
     p. cm.
   Based on the author's Ph.D. thesis presented to the University of Michigan.
   Includes bibliographical references and index.
   ISBN 0-7914-4721-9 (hc : acid-free paper) — ISBN 0-7914-4722 (pb : acid-free paper)
     1. Economic assistance, Domestic—United States—History—20th century. 2.
   Poverty—United States—History—20th century. 3. Dependency—History—20th century. I.
   Title: Civic republican tradition in U.S. poverty policy. II. Title.

   HC110.P6 Z86 2000
   362.5'8'0973—dc21
                                                                              00-026954

10 9 8 7 6 5 4 3 2 1

Contents

Acknowledgments

My wife Marianne deserves first thanks for encouraging me in my endeavors; words cannot express all that I owe to her love and support. I also thank my parents, Frank and Arline Zundel, and my children, Nick and Rachel, for their patience with me at different points in my educational career.

Professor Kim Lane Scheppele, now of the University of Pennsylvania, and Professors John Kingdon (now retired), Mary Corcoran, and Sheldon Danziger of the University of Michigan offered moral support, advice, and criticism in the original production of this work as a Ph.D. dissertation; I thank them all. The Gerald R. Ford Fellowship from the Political Science Department and a Rackham One-Term Dissertation Fellowship from the Graduate School of the University of Michigan supported the research and writing of the dissertation. Research support from the University of Nevada-Las Vegas allowed time for subsequent revisions. I also thank Michael Sherradon and Ray Boshara for taking time to be interviewed for chapter 5. Thanks are also due to the *Policy Studies Journal*; the editors allowed the use of material originally published there.

Finally, I want to thank the people I have known who have experienced poverty in America first hand, several of whom are no longer in this world. They helped me to wake up.

Preface

For a long time welfare reform seemed stuck on the U.S. political agenda like reruns on cable TV. Not only was the issue continually revisited, the language used to discuss it was as predictable as the laugh lines in "I Love Lucy." For over three decades the political discussion of poverty has been dominated by the concept of "welfare dependency," which was also the key term in the debates leading up to the 1996 welfare reform act.

By examining records of congressional debates, Presidential statements, congressional committee hearings and other material, I have traced the roots of the usage of this concept to the civic republican tradition of early America. My central thesis is that many of the conundrums of poverty policy in the twentieth century have been due to the inadequate fit of this tradition in the way it has been adapted to contemporary economic conditions.

The central chapters present the story of how civic republican themes were adapted to public land policy during the first century after the American Revolution, how the symbols of this tradition became implicated in twentieth-century politics, and how contemporary poverty policy has been affected by this heritage. The introductory chapter explains the theory behind this historical interpretation, and the conception of policy analysis that I am applying. (Readers who are more interested in the historical story than in theoretical issues can safely skip that chapter.) The concluding chapter sums up the research findings, examines the problem of rational coherency in the modern use of civic republican themes for poverty policy, and sketches out an alternative policy direction.

My chief aims here are two. One is to find politically acceptable terms in which to justify public policy addressing poverty in this country. The other is to develop a fruitful approach to studying the intersection of ethics and policy. Underlying both of these aims is my belief that policy analysis is best understood as a discipline, not of objective science, but of practical morality.

Declarations
of
Dependency

Chapter 1

Introduction:
Policy Analysis and Ethical Traditions

In the United States, public programs for the poor have been continually pounded by the stormy waves of emotionally charged policy debates. This was most recently demonstrated in the sinking of the federal guarantee of cash aid to mothers with poor children. Despite the new Temporary Assistance for Needy Families program (TANF) and the current economic expansion, the poor are, of course, still with us. Now is the time to draw lessons from the demise of Aid to Families with Dependent Children (AFDC), before the inevitable revisiting of the poverty issue in national politics. The lesson drawn in this work is that policies should be so designed as to successfully navigate the deep-running currents of American beliefs and feelings regarding the poor.

Such deep-running currents are bound up in what are sometimes known as policy "frames." A policy frame is a perspective or viewpoint on a social issue which politicians, the public, and analysts use to make sense of that social issue. Frames are built from culturally powerful symbols existing within a specific political environment:

> Every issue has its own special language and phrases, its characteristic arguments, metaphors, and the like. When events occur that affect policy outcomes, commentary about them

draws on culturally available idea elements and symbols. The ideas in this cultural catalogue are organized and clustered; we encounter them not as individual items but as packages. . . . One can think of the complete *set* of packages that are available for talking about the issue as its "culture."[1]

For example, the symbol of "dependency" has been central to the political discussion of poverty in the United States. This type of symbol and the frame(s) it invokes set the issue within a context of values and beliefs which help shape reactions to the issue; they call attention to some facts rather than others and delimit the types of actions that are appropriate for addressing the issue. A policy frame will also have a history of usage over time, and often over different types of policies. My thesis in this work is that a policy frame inherited from the nineteenth century has significantly affected U.S. poverty policy debates, and that this has created problems for the design of acceptable policies. My aim is to enable the reader to "step back" from this frame by examining it historically, in order to see more clearly its premises, its limitations, and its potential for guiding the design of more acceptable policy programs. For reasons that I will explain further, I call the continued use over time of a particular frame an "ethical tradition."

My original plan did not involve a long historical perspective. I was intrigued by what seemed to me to be a rut in which welfare debates (primarily focussed on AFDC) had been stuck for the last thirty years or so. Continual blanket denunciations of the welfare system had resulted in little but sporadic incremental changes, always in the same direction: a little more money for job search and job training programs, and a little more encompassing requirements for welfare recipients to participate in these programs. However, the reforms never seemed to settle the issue, and the denunciations soon picked up again where they had left off. Whether TANF breaks this pattern is a question I take up in chapter 4, but my hope in setting out was to avoid the rut by examining the frames invoked in these debates and exploring different possibilities for reframing (altering the frames surrounding) the issue of poverty. I began with two case studies, one that I regarded as typical of poverty policy debates and one that seemed more anomalous, intending to analyze and compare the language involved in each of them.[2]

To my surprise, I discovered similarities in the language of the two cases which I came to believe are traceable to the same origin—but rather than the liberal individualism usually discussed by social welfare historians, the origin was an offshoot of the civic republican tradition associated with the period during the American founding. While liberal individualism stresses individual freedom and the limitation of government powers to the protection of individual rights, civic republicanism stresses the virtues that citizens must have in order to be self-governing and the role of the government in supporting or undermining these virtues. As the civic republican tradition is generally considered to have largely died out by the late twentieth century, this discovery changed the focus of the work from a few in-depth case studies to a more extended historical picture of the role of civic republican themes in the shaping of U.S. poverty policies.[3]

The central chapters lay out this historical story. Chapter 2 reviews the origins of civic republicanism in America and the development of its offshoot, agrarian republicanism, up until the early twentieth century. The next three chapters are the heart of the work, showing how the symbols of this tradition have affected three areas of poverty policy debates in the twentieth century: homeownership programs for the poor, cash-aid programs, and ideas for building the capital assets of poor people. The final chapter summarizes the research findings and completes the policy analysis, concluding with some suggestions for reorienting the design of poverty policy programs in the light of these findings. The aim of the research is not so much to extract generalizations about how ethical traditions affect policy processes, but rather to identify and solve a problem in the application of this specific tradition to U.S. poverty policy.

In the rest of this introductory chapter I present the theoretical position underlying my method, albeit in a somewhat roundabout fashion. The first three sections present an intellectual history. In them I circle from the concept of policy frames as used in contemporary policy studies, to the older debate over ideology theory, and then back to the present to show how the use of the concept of ideology in American political science led to the concept of policy frames. This will set the stage for the next three sections by highlighting the problem that is at the heart of my theory: the relation of facts and values in policy analysis. In these sections I argue that it is impossible to exclude values from policy analysis, and that the value-dimension of the ethical traditions used to justify policies can be subjected to rational scrutiny. Nonacademic readers may prefer to skip the rest of this chapter and go on to the historical story beginning in chapter 2.

1. POLICY FRAMES IN POLICY STUDIES

The tactic of examining the language used in policy debates arises from two trends in policy studies linked by the concept referred to above as policy frames, although a variety of terms have been used to express the same general concept.[4] One trend centers on addressing the serious problems of theory and method besetting more traditional forms of policy analysis. The other trend is the use of the concept of policy frames to explain the policymaking process, particularly in the literature on agenda setting. To both introduce the theoretical issues and give a sense of the importance of frames in policymaking, I will begin with a brief summary of this policy process literature.

Much of the current use of the concept of policy frames was inspired by Murray Edelman's writings on how political elites use culturally established symbols for the arousal or quiescence of the mass public, although later authors tended to tone down his implications of cynical manipulation.[5] For example, Roger W. Cobb and Charles D. Elder examined the use of such symbols by activists trying to transfer policy issues from a "systemic" to an "institutional" political agenda, and later brought together a variety of research on how the use of symbols helps to structure the interpretation of inherently ambiguous political information.[6] William A. Gamson is another scholar who followed Edelman's lead. He and his associates explored the linkages between media presentations and popular perceptions of policy issues, focusing on the use of sets of symbols which they call "interpretive packages" composed of (1) framing or pattern-organizing elements such as historical examples, metaphors and catch phrases, and (2) reasoning devices such as appeals to principle and ideas about cause and effect.[7]

This line of thought was further developed in the literature on agenda setting. In John W. Kingdon's landmark work he modeled the agenda setting process as a "garbage can" into which relatively independent "streams" of problem definition, policy idea development, and political situations flow and are occasionally "linked" through the efforts of policy entrepreneurs.[8] Although he only touched on the role of values in the definition of social problems and the emergence of viable policy proposals,[9] the literature discussed above would suggest that the way problems, policies, and politics are joined is through the use of familiar symbols to frame a policy issue. Several authors since have focused attention on the use of symbols in the process of problem definition.[10] In addition, many of those building more general theories of the policy process now stress how particular value-laden viewpoints on a policy issue ("belief systems," "policy images") are used to create the coalitions that dominate particular policy subsystems.[11]

By synthesizing the work described above we can sketch out the relation between policy frames and policymaking. Actors in the policy process draw from a range of culturally familiar symbol-sets (frames) in their attempts to make sense of the social world and to gain or preserve support for the policy ideas they favor. In building political coalitions the affective, emotional associations of these symbols are more important than their cognitive, intellectual associations, but the latter still limit their application and thus advantage those policy ideas to which emotionally powerful symbols can more plausibly be attached. Whenever a policy idea prevails in a political decision the social importance of its associated frame is reinforced, creating a tendency for a particular frame to dominate discussion in an area of policy, and inspiring attempts to adapt it to other issues. Opponents of instituted policies search for alternative frames for interpreting the policy issue from which they can attack the dominant coalition and advance their alternative policies. The end result of this competition is a limited set of policy frames in the public discussion of each issue area, with one of them tending to dominate it at any point in time. In sum, frames are vital in the shaping of public policies.

Beyond the discussion of policy processes, the realization that any policy issue can be (and usually is) interpreted and defined through different frames involving different values and suggesting different solutions has posed a compelling theoretical problem for policy analysts seeking to offer rational advice on policy issues to policymakers. The central issue involves the relation of the analyst to the values embedded in any frame used to interpret a policy issue. Is a "frame neutral" analysis possible? If not, how can the choice of a frame for a policy analysis be justified? But this is not really a new issue, for an older discussion concerning the concept of ideology is the generally unacknowledged grandparent of the current discussion. Reviewing this earlier controversy may help clarify this issue.

2. THE CONCEPT OF IDEOLOGY AND ATTENDANT PROBLEMS

The term "ideology" has had a long, broad and varied use, but a core meaning can be roughly defined. An ideology is some collectively shared system of ideas and values about human beings and society (not necessarily a highly logical and coherent system) which evokes emotional commitment and can be more or less deliberately used to inspire coordinated action and legitimate (or de-legitimate) social institutions and government policies.[12] As can be seen, this is quite similar to the definition of a frame. Knotty problems similarly have been associated with the concept of ideology, regarding its use in explaining social behavior as well as the question of the possibility of nonideological knowledge. The latter question parallels policy analysts' contemporary theoretical concerns about framing.

These problems can be highlighted through a quick look at the origins of the concept. The general claim that various sets of ideas and values influence politics goes back at least as far as Aristotle, who recognized a relation between competing beliefs about justice and conflict between social classes.[13] The modern concept of ideology,[14] however, began with a group of French philosophers in the late eighteenth century who were impressed by the development of British empiricism and Sir Francis Bacon's theory of "idols" (mistaken, irrational conceptions). They held that any ideas incongruent with and not based upon sense impressions—religious and metaphysical beliefs were the primary targets—are socially conditioned distortions of reality which scientific observation should carefully avoid. By doing so, scientists would uncover true knowledge of human behavior which could be used to build a more rational social order. They called their technique "ideology," the science of ideas; it was an epistemological forerunner of the objectivist attempt to separate facts and values in social research. In sum, they believed they held the key to avoiding common but mistaken views of the social world. Ironically, Napoleon turned the tables on these philosophers by calling their "ideology" a deluded and socially destructive system of ideas.

Thus, Karl Marx, while accepting the concept of socially conditioned systems of ideas that obscure reality, used "ideologies" as the term for these distorted systems. He rejected the French philosophers' method for getting at social reality on the grounds that ahistorical sense impressions would only reveal contemporary social arrangements, not the general grounds of human behavior. Marx's historically informed theory was an inversion of that of the German idealist philosopher G. W. F. Hegel, who argued that the different thought systems that characterized particular civilizations were part of an historical unfolding of universal Mind. For Marx, class relations based on the organization of production are the primary basis of social life, conditioning even consciousness; therefore changes in the dominating ideologies reflect changes in the means and modes of production. These dominating ideologies serve to conceal class conflict by justifying class rule. Marx believed his historical analysis of class relations revealed a more objective view of social reality, which had only become possible from the perspective of the imminent end of class rule in history.

When his collaborator, Friedrich Engels, later tried to explicate Marx's ideas, he allowed ideology to provide a causal explanation for people's actions somewhat independent of the socioeconomic causes of behavior. Without this allowance, the assertion that the ideology of a ruling class helped them to control the masses would make no sense; ideology would have no independent motivating force. Reconciling a primary emphasis on the role of class relations based on the mode of production in shaping social behavior with a meaningful role for ideology has been a continuing issue among Marxist theorists.

An alternative perspective came from Max Weber, who broke with Marxism by positing a reciprocal relation between ideological and sociological factors, each having an important effect on the development of the other. Some of his inspiration came from the writings of Frederick Nietzsche, who suggested that all systems of ideas and values are manifestations of a pre-rational will to power. Weber regarded religious or quasi-religious belief systems, expressing a desire to impose order and meaning on the world, to be one of the primary forces shaping different cultures. His method of arriving at causal explanations of social behavior involved using empirical evidence to interpret the subjective state of the individuals involved in collective actions.

Weber conceded that even scientists have an ideological dimension to their thought, as particular sets of ideas and values guide their choice of a subject of study, including which of many potential causal factors are of interest in creating satisfying explanations of facts. Even so, he argued for a fact / value distinction in methodology; while he believed science could help us understand cultural phenomena and thus clarify our own value commitments, he regarded it as powerless to help determine which values were worthy of commitment. Weber's position did not resolve the problem of moral relativism raised by Nietzsche, which was a central issue in the 1920s for German intellectuals grappling with the social disorder of the Weimar Republic. If even scientists and philosophers have an ideological dimension to their thought, how can we judge the relative superiority of different viewpoints? Fierce debates over the relation between reason, science, values, and politics raged between objectivists, Marxists, romantic antirationalists and those still adhering to metaphysics for a standard of values. Such topics should sound familiar to my contemporary academic colleagues.

These issues are directly related to the concept of ideology. The word carries a negative connotation that some systems of belief about the social world are aberrant, yet the grounds for a valid distinction between ideological and nonideological thinking have been controversial. The influence of socioeconomic conditions on thinking is an important part of the concept, but exactly how this works is obscure. One can question whether nonideological thinking is even possible; for example, can "scientific" thinkers escape the influence of social conditions on their thought? And even assuming they can escape social conditioning, can they escape values in order to be fully "objective" and empirical? Or are *all* thought systems regarding the social world rationally arbitrary, based only upon contingent social circumstances and / or "value preferences?" These are the very problems that now trouble contemporary policy analysts and other social scientists.

Karl Mannheim began to address them by building on the work of Weber and that of the Marxist thinker George Lukacs. He accepted that all perspectives on human society, even those of thinkers who aspire to some type of scientific standpoint, are sociologically and historically conditioned. His "sociology of knowledge" proposed to examine the social bases, conditions, and biases of the various forms of human thought systems. Like Weber, Mannheim saw complex relations between ideas and socioeconomic context; unlike Weber, he believed an investigator could discriminate between ideologies by favoring the more comprehensive and coherent viewpoint over the less so.[15] In essence, he was saying that we all hold ideologies, but some can be judged to be better than others—but only in comparison to each other, not in comparison to some absolutely "objective" standpoint, which is impossible for humans to attain. Modern intellectuals happen to be in the best social and historical circumstances to do the work of ideological comparison, synthesis, and refinement, because they are brought together from a variety of social backgrounds from which they become relatively detached.[16] Not long after Mannheim's thesis was put forward, the German intellectual debate was interrupted by the rise to power of the Nazis. After the war similar debates were to occur outside of Germany.

3. AMERICAN POLITICAL SCIENCE: FROM IDEOLOGY TO FRAMES

Apart from Charles Beard's quasi-Marxist early work on the relation between the property holdings and the political thought of the American Founders,[17] there was little sign of any concept of ideology in American political science before the 1920s. Its introduction may be attributed to Charles Merriam and, even more so, to his student Harold D. Lasswell. Lasswell, who had studied Marx, Weber, and Mannheim as well as Freudian psychoanalysis while in Berlin as a graduate student, used the concept of ideology in his argument that political elites exercise power by manipulating the psychological states of the masses. Special symbols (primarily words and combinations of words), because they tap the inner anxieties people have about their social experience, are used by those skilled at this to organize people sharing similar perspectives into groups to support (or attack) the social order. Lasswell hoped that the empirical study of the sources of psychosocial anxieties and the forms of their symbolic expression would be a key to a better world through the scientific understanding of political behavior.[18] One can discern here the original French project of cutting through false systems of thought in order to create a more rational social order.

In the decades from the 1930s to the 1950s the ideologies Lasswell and other American political scientists were worried about were fascism, communism and, for some, McCarthy-style anti-communism. Their defense of liberal democracy against the political movements supported by these systems of thought split into two camps. One camp, heavily influenced by refugee German intellectuals who had experienced the collapse of the Weimar Republic, saw the moral relativism associated with objectivist science and liberal politics as weakening a commitment to the transcendent values that they claimed underlie democratic institutions. They wanted to return to the Western tradition of normative political philosophy and created the political science subfield of political theory, in which the earlier German controversies about relativism, reason, science, values, and politics eventually were to be repeated.

The other camp regarded normative political arguments as part of the problem, and contrasted the conflicts provoked by dogmatic and emotionally charged belief systems with the compromise and stability possible in a system that pragmatically balanced the material interests of the individuals and groups making up the social order. They saw the American political system as a primary example of such a system, and thought it would be best defended by a value-free empirical study of its actual workings.[19] Their position, like Laswell's, mirrored that of the original French "ideologists," in that they believed a scientific and nonideological view of the social world would help create a better society. Some social scientists even claimed that the political quiescence of the American public in the late 1950s heralded an "end of ideology" due to the success of the modern social welfare state in balancing the needs and interests of different social classes.[20] The political theorists' revival of the German debate was delayed, if only temporarily, by the evolution of the second camp into the behavioralist movement which dominated American political science until the social upheavals of the 1960s.

The behavioralists' modeling of the political process as a system for channeling and balancing self-interested behavior (for example, that of voters and interest groups seeking to advance their "interests" and of politicians seeking to gain and retain power) has continued to be an influential approach in American political science; leading examples are versions of interest group pluralism and rational choice theory.[21] One reason such models are attractive is that they simplify a complex reality in such a way as to create testable hypotheses and guide empirical research. However, as it is obvious that people often act against their self-interest (narrowly conceived) because of other motives, criticisms of the shortcomings of such models have accumulated over the years, in particular aimed at their neglect of the role of ideas in motivating political actors.[22] Much as Napoleon criticized the French empiricists, modern critics have also charged that the behavioralists' models are themselves ideological, with roots in the defense of implicit values and particular political arrangements by intellectuals influenced by their social and historical circumstances.[23]

Ensuing attempts to separate and compare the influence of self-interest from the influence of ideas on political behavior have proven futile; they end in a conceptual and methodological morass.[24] For one thing, what you (or any researcher) think is in your or anyone else's "self-interest" is necessarily based on the values and ideas that you hold. An alternative approach to the importance of ideas in political behavior shifted the focus from the motives of political actors to the organizational context in which they act—in short, emphasizing the functions of institutions, including established forms of political language.

Scholars began using language theory to refine the concept of ideology in the 1960s. One who inspired many from other fields was cultural anthropologist Clifford Geertz. Wrestling with the question of how thinking is socially conditioned, he found the two most common answers lacking. The idea that the material interests bound up with a person's social circumstances condition their thinking (for example, in some crude forms of Marxism) reflects either a vague or an overly simplistic psychology. But the more sophisticated (Freudian) alternative theory, that the strains inherent to social life are manifested in emotionally charged thought systems, tends to reduce ideology to emotional expression and thus has trouble explaining its social consequences. According to Geertz, the problem is not that there is no truth in these theories, but that they neglect to link psychological cause to social effect through a theory of symbol formulation; that is, the working out of patterns of meaningfulness in language and other symbolic forms: ". . . what is socially determined is not the *nature* of conception but the *vehicles* of conception [emphasis added] . . . thought consists of the construction and manipulation of symbol systems."[25] Ideologies, then, are symbol systems meant to make problematic social situations meaningful in a way that allows people to act purposefully, and are created through social interaction in specific circumstances; they are not merely an expression of material interests or psychological states.

In American political science the trend in applying language theory to social behavior was carried forward by Edelman, mentioned in section 1 of this chapter, who built upon Lasswell's ideas about symbol usage and mass behavior. I have already reviewed some of the policy process literature pursuing this line of thought. In it the use of terms such as "frames," "interpretive packages," and "belief systems" is clearly an attempt to avoid problematic connotations of the term "ideology," particularly the implication of thinking that is somehow distorted. For on that point, it has become doubtful whether any nonideological perspective is possible. The intellectual history presented above indicates that once it becomes clear that people use frames (ideologies) to interpret the social world, inevitably the problem of a researcher's own frame of interpretation follows. It raises the fundamental question of what it means to do social science.

4. The Non-separability of Facts and Values in Social Research

Attempts to create a value-free, nonideological social science have been rooted in objectivism, a philosophy of science with ancestry in the work of the British and French empiricists with whom I began my story of the concept of ideology. Objectivists assert the validity of knowledge of "objective" phenomena over that of "subjective" experience. The criticisms of objectivism (or, more narrowly, positivism)[26] developed by other writers will not be fully assayed here, but they derive directly from the controversies over the concept of ideology and may be briefly summarized as follows.

Empirical facts do not come to us unmediated; they are only meaningful when interpreted through theoretical concepts, and theories, which are human constructions, are intertwined with values. While a real world places limits on what we can reasonably interpret about what is "out there," there is a huge range of potential experience of that world, and which facts one attends to, how these are named or described, the interpretation of their significance, and what is accepted as convincing explanations of them are all inescapably theoretically mediated. In brief, facts must be interpreted or construed, not merely perceived, in order to be comprehended. The theoretical concepts through which facts are construed are at first acquired through socialization in a particular cultural milieu and incorporate its values, and then may later be elaborated and sometimes changed by an individual pursuing personal purposes, which again involves values. This type of critique has been explicitly applied to the practice of policy analysis, reinforcing the conclusion that an analyst cannot make sense of a policy issue without choosing among policy frames, each based on its own value-laden theory for interpreting social reality.[27] I agree with this assessment.

As an example of how facts and values are intertwined in social research, let's return to American political science. Objectivist researchers such as the behaviorists mentioned above have generally tried to present their work as an empirical, value-free enterprise. The most widely followed research agendas have been set by the concept of democracy, understood as the correspondence of policy decisions to the aggregated preferences of citizens; any goals and values which are democratically set are accepted by researchers as legitimate aims of public policy. By thus attempting to bracket the question of which values are to be preferred, political scientists have turned to empirical questions concerning how well actual political processes translate citizens' preferences into policy decisions (for example, the responsiveness of various political institutions to public opinion, voter behavior or interest group activity), and policy analysts have turned to empirical questions concerning how well policy tools achieve given goals.[28] Actions and consequences, as part of the world of empirical facts, have been regarded as proper subjects of social science research, while goals and values have been considered to be outside the realm of scientific judgment.

Yet whether researchers are aware of it or not, the concept of democracy at the heart of these research agendas reflects the moral theory of utilitarianism and the values that it upholds. For utilitarians, maximizing the sum of individual satisfactions is the ethically correct aim of human behavior. Utilitarians highly value both the individual freedom to choose one's own satisfactions, and satisfying everyone's desires as fully as possible. Research agendas grounded in utilitarian values have likely been carried forward more because they have afforded interesting research topics than because the researchers are convinced that utilitarianism is the most rationally defensible moral theory available, although at one time probably many were so convinced, and some still may be. Although this is not the place to rehearse criticisms of utilitarianism, it should be pointed out that it is far from being universally accepted by moral philosophers.

In contending that any study of human behavior necessarily incorporates particular values,[29] this does not lead me to deny the possibility of intellectual progress on the grounds that all theoretical frames are equally valid or equally invalid. Essentially my position follows Mannheim's belief that we have grounds for preferring some frames over others. For one thing, I think there are empirical reasons to prefer one frame to another. One frame may do a better job of making sense of facts that a rival frame regards as problematic.

In the case of the political science research agendas mentioned above, the accumulation of empirical knowledge guided by this research paradigm has led some social scientists to critically reexamine its underlying assumptions.[30] For example, public opinion studies have demonstrated that, in general, most citizens' policy preferences are relatively uninformed and unstable.[31] Thus, it is quite plausible that political institutions create, shape, or manipulate preferences rather than simply respond to them. Furthermore, no actual political process aggregates preferences in any straightforward sense, except preferences concerning which political candidates should hold office. Ranking the multitude of political values or policy aims cannot be reduced to such a clear-cut decision. It may be a more accurate description of actual democratic processes to say that people charge their governmental representatives, not with aggregating individual preferences, but with discovering, forming, or promoting a collective preference. That is, citizens do not assess government actions simply by the satisfaction of their individual preferences, but by the conformance of these actions with widely shared conceptions of social purposes and values.[32]

Facing such evidence, the utilitarian conception of democracy as the aggregation of individual citizens' preferences comes into focus as a problem, and an alternative conception of democracy (or some other guiding concept) becomes vital to the continuance of research. For example, democracy can be conceived as public deliberation aimed at practical agreements based on some rational conception of the common good. This is an alternative frame, based on different values, and it implies a whole different research agenda.[33] In fact, it underlies the research presented here, which was conceived of as a contribution towards such public deliberation in the area of poverty policy.

But in addition to empirical considerations, unlike both objectivists on the one side and postmodernist, Nietzschean relativists on the other, I do not regard value judgments as outside the realm of rational thinking. I believe that frames can be fruitfully compared with one another on both empirical *and* ethical grounds, and that this is a legitimate and important task for social scientists and other scholars. I will defend the rationality of value judgments after the following section, in which I begin to lay out my own views on the issues that I have been raising. I hope that the question I want to answer is by now clear, although it may sound paradoxical: through what frame should we (researchers) view the frames through which we (humans) view the social world?

5. ETHICAL TRADITIONS

In broad terms the aim of my research, as indicated above, is to contribute to public deliberation towards practical agreement on policies reflecting a rational conception of the common good. My method is to identify and critically examine the contemporary use, in policy discourse, of what thus far have been called "ideologies" or "frames." This method builds on the work of those applying language theory to the concept of ideology, and I accept their general picture of the role of language in policy processes. But my orientation towards this phenomenon is not neutral; if the term "ideology" has unacceptable negative connotations, I find the current alternatives unacceptably non-evaluative. That is, they convey little about one's position on the key theoretical issues, particularly one's attitude towards the value-dimension of frames (interpretive packages, belief systems, etc.). Therefore I have coined my own term, "ethical traditions," in order to highlight two aspects of my perspective which might otherwise be obscured. The first involves the human capacity for independent thinking, and the second involves the relation between reason and values.

First, the term "tradition" is meant to convey not only continuity over time in the use of a set of framing symbols, but that such continuity is due to the ongoing use of a shared cultural resource—in this case, language—and not to any presumed rigidities in the nature of thinking. I reject the idea that symbol systems persist because people have little control over the content of their minds—for example, that thinking has little or no independence from socioeconomic context and / or subconscious motivations. No doubt social context and subconscious motivations affect thinking to various degrees in different individuals, but I would argue that thinking can also be, and often is, a creative act which moves away from such limitations. Although the given symbols associated with a tradition do have limits to their intelligible usage, people can exercise some degree of creative freedom in adapting them to various purposes and circumstances. People vary not only in terms of cognitive sophistication and affective orientations towards ethical traditions, but also in terms of how rigid or flexible they are when they reproduce them. To put it plainly, people don't just learn and then express traditions in a mechanical fashion, sometimes they "play" with them in the process. This is true of the use of a language more generally; even though people are constrained by the words handed on to them, sometimes they make up new words or use old words in new ways. When a policy actor adapts an established ethical tradition to new circumstances and / or attaches it to a new policy idea, this is a creative act, and as such is one of the more unpredictable aspects of the policy process.

Clearly people in certain social environments are better situated to accomplish the creative adaptation of ethical traditions. People who are active in modern-day politics are exposed to multiple traditions, making them more conscious of their use, and they have incentives to rework them in ways that suit their needs and purposes.[34] This parallels Mannheim's argument about the social environment of intellectuals. He pointed out that intellectuals are exposed to multiple ideologies and have the time, training, and incentives to rework them into more comprehensive and coherent forms. Mannheim hoped that intellectuals would take on the function of ideological comparison, synthesis, and refinement, and I am similarly proposing the examination of ethical traditions for a more conscious, coherent, and effective usage in guiding our social decisions. The term "political traditions" would also work, but I use the modifier "ethical" instead as a positive way of emphasizing the normative character of these traditions, the fact that they involve the question of what our moral aims as a society ought to be. Discussions of moral aims are viewed here as a normal, necessary, and desirable component of political discussions, whether conducted by scholars or anyone else, and not set in opposition to some allegedly value-free style of thought and discourse about politics.

In sum, my position on some of the key questions first raised by the concept of ideology is that scientific thinking can and should be relatively free from social conditioning, but not from values. It does not differ from ordinary thinking on either of these grounds (some "ordinary" people are very unconventional thinkers), but by ideally being more careful, self-conscious, logical and well informed (gathering and accounting for empirical evidence remains an important task). Critically examining the ethical traditions used in policy discussions, as well as being self-consciously critical of our larger theoretical orientations (which may be called "ethical traditions" within social science), are important tasks for social scientists and other scholars. But in these tasks, as for all humans thinking about our social life, facts and values are intertwined. This intertwining of facts and values need not threaten the idea of scientific progress, as this kind of "bias" is only a problem if there are no criteria for choosing among competing value-laden perspectives. For at the bottom of the desire to separate facts and values is the question of the rationality of different value priorities, and of the ethical theories which articulate them.

6. The Rationality of Ethics

The question of the rationality of ethics has been raised here in two distinct but related ways. One issue is that of the possibility of scientific progress if our theories are necessarily intertwined with values; this stems from the problem all researchers face of offering rational grounds for their choice among social theories to use in their research. The second is the issue more specific to my project, deriving from my version of ideology theory, which is that of evaluating the ethical traditions that are used in the public discussion of a specific policy issue. The solution to the question of the rationality of ethics that will be proposed is relevant to both of these issues, but it will be extensively applied (in the rest of this book) only in my analysis of an ethical tradition used in poverty policy. To apply it to the defense of the larger theoretical framework guiding my analysis would be a book in itself, so here I have only been able to sketch out the direction my argument would take.[35]

The widespread skepticism in our society towards the rationality of ethics is historically rooted in the overthrow of natural law theory from a position of dominance in Western philosophy. Traditional natural law theorists held (and hold) that there are fundamental principles of right and wrong that apply to all human beings, are grounded in human nature and its proper ends, and are knowable through the exercise of human reason. The violent breakup of Christendom after the rise of Protestantism, the exploration of foreign cultures beyond Europe, and a growing awareness of social change over time eventually weakened the religious underpinnings and cast doubt on the universality of what was taken to be the natural moral order. The objectivist response to this situation was articulated by David Hume's is / ought distinction in which he argued that while empirical knowledge (knowledge of what is) is based on reason, morality (knowledge of what ought to be) is based on sentiments.[36]

Jeremy Bentham, the father of utilitarianism, was one of many people who tried to lay a new basis for a moral theory based on reason. He began with the foundational principle of maximizing human happiness: accepting that people have irrational preferences for some things over others, one should think rationally, that is, instrumentally, about how best to satisfy these preferences. Moral action, in this view, is that which produces the most aggregate satisfaction (utility) to humanity.[37] Modern science has been heir to the view that evaluative statements are the expression of nonrational individual preferences, and utilitarianism has had a wide influence in the social sciences, particularly economics.[38] I have already discussed the impact of utilitarianism on research agendas in political science.

Other moral theories starting with different foundational principles have competed with utilitarianism, notably theories of human rights and / or obligations such as that of Immanuel Kant, but the inconclusiveness of these debates led to even greater skepticism about the rationality of moral theorizing. The ultimate expression of such skepticism came from Nietzsche, who suggested that all ethical theories are expressions of a pre-rational will to power. His postmodernist, anti-objectivist followers would "deconstruct" all statements about reality to exhibit the implicit values they uphold as well as the rational arbitrariness of those values, thus discrediting both scientific objectivity and moral absolutes together. Their ostensible purpose is to emancipate human beings from such intellectual constrictions, but to emancipate *for* what is a difficult question for them. In response, objectivists have redoubled their insistence on the separability of facts and values for fear of a descent into unreason. In my view, however, anxiety to protect the role of reason in human affairs from postmodernist attacks is unwarranted, as even deconstructionists go on reasoning about the world and the choices they face. The way forward, rather, is the reconstruction of rational moral discussion.

Alasdair MacIntyre is one of those pursuing this answer to the modern intellectual dilemma.[39] He has argued that the multiple views of justice prevalent in our society (based variously, for example, on utility, or dessert, or inalienable rights), and the different conceptions of practical rationality connected to these views (the costs and benefits of consequences, impartiality, achieving an ultimate good), are cultural fragments which we have inherited, the remnants of more coherent philosophical traditions from earlier cultures. Older traditions such as versions of Aristoteleanism and Augustinianism were abandoned by many intellectuals at the time of the Enlightenment for the project of rebuilding moral theory upon first principles undeniable to any rational person. It was the historical failure to establish such self-evident first principles (as attempted in both utilitarianism and Kantian theory) that sealed the loss of faith in rational argumentation about ethics.

But according to MacIntyre, if you reject the false expectations of this Enlightenment project you can avoid the disillusionment that leads to ethical irrationalism. MacIntyre proposed a conception of rational inquiry as embodied in traditions. In this conception, standards of rational justification are not based on self-evident first principles. They emerge from and are part of a history in which they are vindicated (or fail to be vindicated) by the way in which they transcend the limitations of and provide remedies for the defects of their predecessors within that same history. Enlightenment rationalism as an approach to moral theory was itself born this way, offering a standard of justification meant to overcome the problems associated with the earlier natural law traditions. MacIntyre argues that this Enlightenment project has failed to vindicate itself.

Instead of continuing to pursue the project of justification by self-evident first principles, he would have justification take the form of a narrative of the historical course of the development of a tradition. First principles are not justified independently, but as part of the rational superiority of a whole theoretical structure over all previous attempts within that tradition to formulate such principles. To be rational means to participate in and identify with the history culminating in the construction of a particular theoretical structure. It is only in relation to a competing theory or set of theories that a theory can be justified. The success or failure of the whole theory in meeting objections from within or without the tradition is what vindicates or fails to vindicate the first principles.

Building on Mannheim's approach to evaluating ideologies, MacIntyre has proposed the use of an historical argument to understand, compare, and evaluate moral traditions. His method offers the hope of progress in rational moral theory. I have modeled my own research along these lines, replacing MacIntyre's focus on intellectual history with a focus on the history of public discourse within a particular policy area. (I have also modeled this theoretical chapter along these lines, using an historical argument to justify my theoretical approach.)

To fully assess the relative superiority of the ethical traditions associated with poverty policy, I would have to compare them against one another (in particular, modern liberalism versus civic republicanism) in terms of such criteria as their comprehensiveness (in organizing the facts and values claimed by various parties to be relevant to the issue), coherence (of the internal logic of the tradition and in its appropriateness to the situation), and consensus (the ability to generate a course of action to which people will agree, thus satisfying our proximate aim of cooperative social action). But as I have come to believe that a version of civic republicanism has dominated this policy area, I have chosen for this study the more manageable task of examining how well this particular tradition maintained coherence while adapting to the challenges of changing social conditions. In the concluding chapter I will stand within the republican tradition and make some policy suggestions intended to overcome its problems of coherency.

7. CONCLUSION

Before turning to my research, it may be helpful to conclude this chapter by comparing my approach to those of others who are attempting to move beyond the critique of objectivist conceptions of policy analysis and create new theories and methods. All of these efforts are in their early stages, but two of the most advanced that I am aware of are those of Martin Rein and Frank Fischer.

Rein examined the different ways analysts might relate to policy frames, and proposed a "value-critical" policy analysis which would ferret out the frames underlying public policies as a prelude to frame criticism, frame building, and frame integration.[40] My theoretical views grew out of reflection on Rein's, but my method is different. In his early work he explored puzzles in the relation between policy design and policy practice, and more recently he and his collaborator Donald Schön have conducted empirical studies of cases of frame conflict to determine conditions which facilitate the successful reframing of policy issues.[41] I have focused on the language of policy debates, and use history to create critical distance from the frames revealed in this language.[42] By examining the use of an ethical tradition over time and changing conditions, I can then apply an evaluative criteria concerning the "fit" of the tradition to modern circumstances.

Fischer has developed a schematic of four "discursive phases" in the discussion of policy issues, in which emphasis from phase to phase shifts from empirical to normative issues. He thus admits a variety of methods as appropriate to different phases of inquiry.[43] I am very sympathetic to his effort to divide up the logic of inquiry into different phases this way, each with its own characteristic methods. My research here fits his description of the "situational validation" phase of policy discourse: an inquiry into the fit between a normative framework and a particular situation regarded as a social problem. Fischer does not prescribe a particular method for this phase of inquiry, but indicates that it is most compatible with the "interpretive" schools of social science such as social phenomenology, symbolic interactionism, and ethnomethodology.[44] He is explicit that his overall aim is an "emancipatory" social science that would aid policy actors in understanding, and presumably gaining control over, the ways they make and remake their social world.[45] I am in concurrence with this emancipatory aim, but would go further to say that we are to be emancipated from uncritical adherence to ethical traditions in order to then commit ourselves to our critically arrived at best understanding of ethical social aims and actions. To "deliberate" (de-liberate) literally means to move the will from freedom to a conscious commitment to a particular course of action.

As one step, then, in this process of emancipation and deliberation, the chapters that follow describe the long use of a particular ethical tradition which has played an important role in promoting several different policy ideas in the United States. It is the story of civic republicanism as it was adapted to nineteenth-century public land policies and from there to various usages in twentieth-century poverty policy. The central symbols of this tradition are the words "dependence" and "independence," symbols with important intellectual and emotional associations that take us back to the very birth of this nation.

Chapter 2

Dependence and Independence
in the Nineteenth Century

One of the most familiar words in U.S. poverty policy debates is "dependency." This chapter traces the American political use of the word back to English ideas about dependent classes, adapted to a new environment in which the majority of adult males were property-owning farmers. The leaders of the American Revolution built on this rhetorical ground with the language of civic republicanism, which emphasized the association of property ownership, independence and civic virtue on the one hand, and poverty, dependence and moral and social corruption on the other. From this, in turn, came a tradition of agrarian republicanism, which held that owning and working a piece of land gives a person the economic independence and the character traits needed to fulfill the role of responsible citizen, and thus that government should make property ownership available to the mass of the citizenry. These principles became a standard part of American political language during the nineteenth century, supporting as aims of public policy the creation of opportunities for poor Americans to become independent property owners and the disciplining of those poor who remained dependent. The chapter concludes by noting the passing of the social conditions in which this ethical tradition had coherence.

1. Dependence in an Independent Society

Dependency was an accepted fact of life in England during the seventeenth and eighteenth centuries. Each person had a "place and station" linked by increments of subordination to those above and below them in the social hierarchy. But the many social ranks were also divisible into two broader categories: "gentlemen," composed of the gentry on up through the gradations of the nobility, and "commoners," from yeoman farmers down to the servants and slaves at the bottom rungs. These two categories were widely regarded by those on the upper rung as defining different types of beings, possessing different mental, emotional, and physical natures. Basic to the distinction, however, was that gentlemen were relatively independent in this world of dependencies; wealth gave them freedom from want, freedom from ignorance, and freedom from manual labor.[1]

Physical labor was particularly identified with the condition of dependence and servility. Commoners were thought to need to work not only to supply their necessities, but also to discipline their character and keep them from idleness and its associated vices, to which they were thought to be especially prone.[2] As they had little possibility of owning land, the primary source of wealth at the time, most commoners were dependent upon obeying the will of some landlord or master who provided the means of their support. Without such attachments they would certainly be subject to severe poverty; more importantly, when thus detached from steady work and the supervision of their social superiors they were regarded as dangerous: servile in character yet without needed discipline. It was this view of the able-bodied unemployed that made forced labor a policy emphasis.

English society had long had provisions for the impoverished. During the Middle Ages the Christian duty to give aid to the poor had been carried out through guilds, monasteries and, most especially, local parishes. As the church was a public institution and its tithes a form of tax, the emerging state of the sixteenth century easily assimilated the parish system of poor relief. But as a changing economy began uprooting people from traditional feudal attachments, the consequent increase in landless and masterless men swelled the number of beggars, thieves, and vagabonds, creating serious concerns about the threat to social order. Parliament in a number of acts not only upgraded the system of local relief for those poor who were physically or mentally unable to work, but it also sought through various means to force the able-bodied poor to labor. The aim was both to relieve poverty and to reinforce social discipline. The Elizabethan Poor Law of 1601 brought these acts together in a systematic form which stood relatively unchanged for two centuries in England, and provided the pattern for the poor laws of the American colonies.[3]

Life in the colonies reflected life in the mother country, but with significant differences. The Poor Law system of local relief with separate provisions for the "impotent" and able-bodied (later, "worthy" and "unworthy") poor was copied in the colonies despite the notable difference that the able-bodied unemployed were less of a problem due to the abundance of land. There was not the huge mass of indigents common to European societies; in the colonies the concentrations of unemployed were in the urban port cities where many were en route to other parts. The vast majority of white adult males owned their own land. In the mid-1700s unpropertied laborers comprised less than a third of the population (excluding slaves, women, and children), a great many of these being recent immigrants and young men who hadn't yet established themselves. In England the proportion of propertied to unpropertied was the reverse.[4]

Still, the greater need and opportunity for labor helped keep the stigma on the character of the able-bodied unemployed at least as serious as it was in England. In the colonies, however, it was not because they were dangerously idle commoners, it was simply because they were idle. The Calvinist emphasis on the virtue of hard work was widespread, as were citations of the biblical maxim that those who would not work should not eat. While the colonists did much to care for neighbors in temporary distress, the disabled, orphans, and widows with children, men regarded as voluntarily idle were punished by being bound out as indentured servants, whipped and run out of town, jailed, or, eventually, confined to workhouses.[5]

The fine calibrations of dependence present in England were not sustainable in the colonies, nor was labor unequivocally associated with dependency. Most of the white adult males were freeholding "yeoman" (freeman) farmers—commoners in that they worked with their hands, yet independent in that they owned their land relatively free of feudal obligations. The higher ranks of the nobility were not present, and those who tried to appropriate the status of gentry (untitled, but educated and of independent financial means) found it difficult to support themselves without engaging in some kind of pecuniary activity, usually commerce or a professional occupation. Thus the preponderance of white adult males were of relatively equal condition, "independent" yet supporting themselves through some type of labor. Below them on the social scale were the slaves and indentured servants. These were the "dependent," like women and children a kind of property with few or no political rights. Their dependency was conspicuous and their treatment, compared to practice in England, unusually brutal and humiliating. By the mid-1700s this preeminent line of social status between dependence and independence had become stark, and the onus of dependency severe.[6] Under these conditions, the traditional English scorn for the unemployed poor as servile characters in need of discipline became intertwined with the American opprobrium against dependency in an independent society.

2. A LANGUAGE OF INDEPENDENCE: CIVIC REPUBLICANISM

Underlying the colonial contempt was the assumption that such indigents were responsible for their condition, that they could fairly easily obtain employment and eventually gain land and economic independence if they were willing to discipline themselves and work. There was some truth in this view, at least in the early colonial period. Early on the attempt to maintain a privileged control of land, difficult anyway on the frontier of a vast continent, had given way to widespread ownership as the most effective spur to economic development; the royal favorites and chartered companies first granted ownership by the king discovered that cultivation was best induced by parceling out their land to individual families. The New England townships turned to individual ownership as it was found to be both more productive than cultivation in common and more compatible with the Puritan work ethic. It was assumed that the corollary of "those who do not work should not eat" was that those who worked should reap rewards in proportion to their effort, which in effect meant that they should own the land they labored on. Outside of New England all of the colonies at one time or another offered "headrights" of certain amounts of acreage to settlers on very favorable terms, sometimes with seeds, tools, stock, and other supplies thrown into the bargain. Even indentured servants were eligible for headrights when their period of service was completed.[7]

Compatible social ideas developed reciprocally with the condition of widespread landownership, particularly in service to the political need of the yeomen class to protect their land tenure from the threats of gentlemen with aristocratic ambitions.[8] One such idea was that widespread ownership, because of the independent citizens it produced, was the foundation of a truly virtuous society, and that the European settlement of America was divinely ordained to demonstrate this truth. A favorite biblical quotation in New England election day sermons was Micah's prophetic vision of the New Jerusalem, in which each man would be able to sit under his own "vine and fig tree."[9] As another example, the monopolization of land in large, uncultivated holdings was frequently attacked on the moral grounds that the property exceeded the "need and use" of its legal owners, and thus illegitimately restricted the opportunity for others to utilize the land.[10]

Colonists were particularly receptive to English philosophical currents justifying a labor right of property and widespread landownership. John Locke's late seventeenth-century work, *Two Treatises of Government*, was widely quoted in the colonies, as is well-known.[11] Locke argued that government is based on a social contract between individuals for the purpose of protecting natural rights to life, liberty, and property. The natural right of property is in effect once a person mixes his labor with natural resources, subject to the proviso that he leave "as much and as good" for others to utilize. Less well-known today is James Harrington's *The Commonwealth of Oceana*, which was also widely read in America during the century and a half after its first publication in 1656.[12] Harrington argued that the form of government that most closely approached the public interest was that of a Republic founded on popular participation, in which the mass of the people shared constitutional power with an elected elite of superior talent. More importantly, he held that because property ownership is the foundation of political power, a stable government of this form could only be built upon a condition of widespread property ownership.[13] Following the classical view that property ownership and the country life are the foundations of civic virtue, Harrington assumed that a society of numerous landholders would also be a society of exceptional civic virtue. His book set forth, in utopian guise, a program for such a society. One of his fundamental constitutional devices was an "agrarian law" aimed at maintaining widespread property ownership, such as by requiring large estates to be divided between the deceased owner's family members rather than passing to the eldest male.[14]

As the independence of property ownership was equated with virtue, propertyless dependency symbolized vice. During the decade of crisis preceding the American Revolution, the many strands of colonial polit-ical language—biblical, Lockean, Harringtonian and others—became incorporated into, or dominated by, a pervasive political idiom in which the association of dependency with moral and social corruption was a central element. Adopted from the early eighteenth-century English opposition "party," it portrayed political life as the constant struggle between citizens' desire for liberty and rulers' lust for power. The inde-pendence of property owners was seen as the foundation of public-spir-ited virtue, but rulers when unchecked sought to corrupt citizens by bringing them into financial and thus political dependence. This ethical tradition, known as civic republicanism, was used by colonial activists to define the meaning of contemporary political events. They claimed that a power-hungry government ministry was destroying the balance of the English constitution and seeking to bring citizens into a state of abject dependency, or "slavery" as they so often put it. New taxes, for example, were construed not merely as a financial burden, but as part of a plot to attack the colonists' property and economic independence.[15]

It was a time of unnerving social change in the colonies, due primar-ily to a ballooning, ambitiously mobile population and the rapid exten-sion of the market. Traditional social relations were breaking down at the same time that individual opportunities were harder to find. Parliament tried to close off the frontier because of problems of safety and political control, and transients swelled the number of poor in many areas and strained the poor law system of local relief. Uncertain of sustaining the exceptionally egalitarian and prosperous conditions prevailing in America as compared to Europe, many colonists worried about falling back into the dread state of poverty and dependence.[16] The Whig gentlemen who composed the colonies' political elite shaped such anxieties into a nation-alist movement, using a familiar political language to mobilize the yeomen.[17] As midwives to the birth of the new nation, civic republican conceptions of poverty and dependence, property and independence, were to leave a long-lasting mark on its political language.

3. CREATING INDEPENDENT CITIZENS: AGRARIAN REPUBLICANISM

The Revolutionary War, like other wars at other times, accelerated currents of social change. Not only did demographic and economic changes continue, but the language of the Revolution was put to unanticipated purposes. The pamphleteering revolutionary leaders had expanded the sphere of public political discourse and shared with common people a set of symbols whose meaning could be contested.[18] These symbols were used to channel energies not just towards political independence but into attacks against deference and dependency within the new nation. Common people challenged the "natural" political leadership of the gentry, and the institutions of indentured servitude and slavery were increasingly called into question.[19] Civic republican language could also be used to defend slavery, however, by characterizing African-Americans as of an inferior and naturally dependent race whose freedom in a republican nation would be a source of corruption. Similarly, the non-slave poor were depicted as individuals of dependent character unfit for the full rights of citizenship.[20]

The growth in the numbers of such poor in the crowded coastal areas was profoundly troubling to many political leaders, who saw life without work, or with monotonous and poorly paid wage labor, as contributing to the dependent, stunted character imputed to these people. Their ideal was the hardworking, enterprising, liberty-loving freehold farmer, whose circumstances and manner of life were assumed to promote the virtues necessary for the responsible exercise of citizenship. (The smaller class of artisans and mechanics who produced "necessary and useful" goods and could aspire to owning their own shops was in a somewhat similar condition of life, and thus secondarily acceptable as republican citizens.) Many saw the expansion of urban poverty as a sign of a society in which population had begun to outrun available land, resulting in movement from an agricultural economy to one dominated by commerce and non-household manufacturing. Such a movement was thought to have plunged European societies into a pit of vices ensuing from the luxury of the rich and the degradation of the poor. Some Americans saw this as underlying the political corruption of England, and were determined to avoid the mother country's fate by broadening access to land for the masses.[21]

Mirroring Harrington's fictional Oceana with its laws to maintain widespread property ownership, the believers in a virtuous republic of independent farmers (as well as those who wanted land for themselves) fought feudal forms of inheritance and sought to open new land to settlement. Several of the new state constitutions affirmed a "right to acquire" property as well as to hold it,[22] and, during the writing of the

Virginia Constitution, Thomas Jefferson proposed that persons not owning at least fifty acres of land be granted enough to raise their holdings to
that minimum. Although that proposal failed, he continued his attack on
the concentration of property ownership as state representative and as governor by opposing entails and primogeniture.[23] Virginia and most of the
other states soon provided for dividing estates more equally among surviving sons, daughters, and widows, and abolished feudal forms of land
tenure.[24] But the chief issue in land policy was the huge public domain on
the western frontier, surrendered by the states to the national government.

There was general agreement that sales of the public lands would be
used to pay the war debt, but the manner of sale was controversial. Those
of like mind with Jefferson, agrarian republicans who envisioned a nation
of property-owning farmers selling grain on the world market, wanted
easy access to public land for new settlement.[25] However, European
restrictions on international trade caused U.S. agricultural surpluses and
unemployment during the half-decade following the war, challenging this
agrarian vision. One response, to be spearheaded by James Madison, was
to work for more reciprocal international trade relations. Others, including Alexander Hamilton, broke with agrarianism to promote finance and
manufacturing within the United States as the key to employment and
national economic independence. Concerned about controlling the pace
of emigration from the eastern states and insuring adequate government
revenues, the Hamiltonians generally preferred sales of large tracts at high
prices. Leaders from both positions cooperated in creating the strengthened national government of the new Constitution which was needed to
pursue either program, but their differences came to the fore during
Washington's presidency.[26]

Congress under the Articles of Confederation had adopted a system
of auctioning tracts of various sizes, with minimum price requirements
and reserved plots for veterans and educational purposes, and later
amended it to provide for sales on credit. With cheap land still available
in the states, however, early results were disappointing and led to ill-fated
special sales of huge tracts to speculative companies. These bad experi-
ences caused a halt in sales for several years after the ratification of the
Constitution in 1787, but lobbying for small unit sales, preemption rights
for squatters, and even free land soon began to grow.[27] The claim was
made that the restrictive land policy was meant to avoid depopulating the
eastern states, and was anti-republican because it forced the poor to
become a dependent class:

Consider that many of your citizens are destir ite of the comforts, nay, the common necessaries of life, without a prospect of providing for the subsistence of themselves and families: I ask, would Congress prevent the emigration of such persons if they could? . . . I question if any man would be hardy enough to point out a class of citizens by name, that ought to be the servants of the community, yet, unless that is done, to what class of the people could you direct such a law? But if you passed such an act, it would be tantamount to saying that there is some class which must remain here, and by law must be obligated to serve the others for such wages as they please to give.[28]

When revenue considerations finally reopened the public land issue near the end of Washington's second term, most of the congressional debate centered on the practical effect of various possible provisions,[29] but the question of selling smaller tracts (160 *vs.* 640 acres) drew forth republican declamations:

> . . . it would accommodate, as much as possible, the poorer class of their citizens . . . to be put into a situation in which they might exercise their own will, which they would not be at liberty to do if they were obliged to become tenants to others. To live in that dependent way had a tendency to vitiate and debase their minds, instead of making them free, enlightened, and independent. . . . [They] would be enabled to become possessed of real property—a situation incident to freedom, and desired by all . . . the peace, and happiness, and attachment of the people would be more likely to be secured, when the land was occupied by real proprietors, than if possessed by persons who were subject, by being tenants, to the will of others.[30]

> The dividing of lands into small lots would put it into the possession of real proprietors, and have a tendency to make good Republicans instead of servile tenants dependent upon tyrannical landlords.[31]

But the Hamiltonian forces had the upper hand at this point, and killed the plan for smaller unit sales in the Senate. The Land Act of 1796 as passed doubled the minimum price per acre and provided for only very restrictive credit. Agitation for easier terms, smaller unit sales, and curtailing speculation mushroomed during the increasingly partisan controversies which marked President Adam's term, culminating in the fight over the Harrison Land Act of 1800. With this act the proponents of agrarian republicanism finally won smaller unit sales, liberalized credit, and preemptive rights to buy at the minimum price for squatters who had developed public land before the passage of the act. The political forces behind this act also helped carry Jefferson into the presidency that same year.[32]

Land policy was but one of the issues that divided Hamiltonian "Federalists" and Jeffersonian "Republicans," but it was integral to the Republican program. The Republicans revitalized the language of the Revolution in their efforts to mobilize the farm vote and unite local political factions into a national constituency, characterizing Federalist policies as the design of centralizing aristocrats plotting anew to reduce citizens to a degrading dependency. Republican independence and virtue were claimed to be at stake, and to depend upon remaining a nation predominated by property-owning farmers. These familiar themes were combined with the increasingly popular language, growing with the extension of market relations, of a more individualistic Lockean liberalism in which citizens used their independence to pursue prosperity and private happiness rather than for self-sacrificing public service.[33]

With the Harrison Act and President Jefferson's Louisiana Purchase of 1803, the agrarian republican program seemed to have wide horizons; however, the old problems of restricted international trade and periodic agricultural surpluses continued to bedevil it. The war with England in 1812 was a turning point, leading even Jeffersonians to endorse the development of manufacturing in order to enlarge the domestic market. Senator Henry Clay's "American System" of protective tariffs, internal improvements, and a national bank, a reincarnation of the Hamiltonian program, gained wide support in the postwar years.[34] But these same years marked another turning point. Before 1812 sales of the public lands were steady but modest, slowed by "Indian" troubles and competition with cheap land sold by the old states and private companies. After the war, with booming agricultural prices and the defeat of aboriginal resistance, settlers began flooding into the Mississippi Valley.[35] The rapid growth of the west set off several decades of political competition and shifting alliances between East and West, and North and South, and the language of agrarian republicanism was kept alive in service to the west's interest in developing the public lands.

An early period of rapidly rising land prices inevitably ended in a depression, precipitating reform of the credit system of land sales.[36] Participants in the debate over the Land Act of 1820, which mandated cash-only sales, continually drew on the ideal of the virtuous independent farmer to distinguish the interests of "good" settlers from those of "bad" speculators. Actually both farmers and politicians engaged in speculation, but the rhetoric aimed to lend the still-potent halo of Jefferson's creed to competing proposals.[37] Over the next couple of decades Senator Thomas Hart Benton of Missouri propagated the agrarian republican language along with his proposals to reduce the price of unsold public lands. Finally, playing Jefferson to cast Presidential challenger Henry Clay as Hamilton, President Andrew Jackson sanctioned the use of this language for the newly forming Democratic Party of the mid-1800s.[38]

> The freeholder . . . is the natural supporter of a free government, and it should be the policy of republics to multiply their freeholders, as it is the policy of monarchies to multiply tenants. We are a republic, and we wish to continue so: then multiply the class of freeholders; pass the public lands cheaply and easily into the hands of the People; sell, for a reasonable price, to those who are able to pay; and give, without price, to those who are not. . . . It brings a price above rubies—a race of virtuous and independent farmers, the true supporters of their country, and the stock from which its best defenders must be drawn. (Sen. Benton)[39]

> The wealth and strength of a country are in its population, and the best part of that population are the cultivators of the soil. Independent farmers are everywhere the basis of society, and the true friends of liberty. . . . [Land policy should] afford every American citizen of enterprise the opportunity of securing an independent freehold . . . (Pres. Jackson)[40]

4. DISCIPLINING THE DEPENDENT: REFORMING PUBLIC RELIEF

Though the tenets of agrarian republicanism had become standards of American political language by the Jacksonian era, changing political and economic conditions continued to challenge their application. The right to vote was increasingly extended to satisfy the demands of farmers leasing property, artisans, and mechanics. Thus, in order to cover a viable national coalition, the "real people" whom Jackson defended against the aristocratic forces of corruption were broadened into a more general "producing class" and not limited to property-owning farmers. The tension between the more conservative conception and the Jacksonian position can be seen evolving in the debates over extending the franchise in the state constitutional conventions of the 1820s:[41]

> The great body of the people, are now the owners and actual cultivators of the soil. With that wholesome population we always expect to find moderation, frugality, order, honesty, and a due sense of independence, liberty, and justice. It is impossible that any people can lose their liberties by internal fraud or violence, so long as the country is parcelled out among freeholders of moderate possessions, and those freeholders have a sure and efficient control in the affairs of the government . . . I wish those who have an interest in the soil, to retain the exclusive possession of a branch in the legislature . . .[42]

> . . . many, though not proprietors, are yet cultivators of the soil: others are engaged in avocations of a different nature, often as useful, presupposing no less integrity, requiring as much intelligence, and as fixed a residence, as agricultural pursuits. Virtue, intelligence, are not among the products of the soil. Attachment to property, often a sordid sentiment, is not to be confounded with the sacred flame of patriotism.[43]

Despite the efforts to create a nation of independent citizens, the number of "dependent" Americans continued to grow. Tenant farming never disappeared, as many freeholders, loaded with debt and living a precarious economic existence, lost their property after being struck by sickness, accidents, drought, or falling agricultural prices. Their claim on the right to vote was difficult to oppose. However, the idea of extending the franchise to paupers, factory wage workers or free African-Americans had much less support; dependency was still a live issue in these cases.[44] Aside from the worries of Northerners about the extension of slavery into the new territories, the most troubling growth in dependency continued to be the number of wage earners and unemployed in the constantly expanding urban centers.

In England, concentrations of such poor provided low-wage labor to manufacture competitively priced exports for a favorable balance of trade. Under the Poor Law's emphasis on forced labor for the able-bodied, by the end of the eighteenth century English authorities were gathering paupers together for small-scale manufacturing. Thus, the early factories were associated with workhouses for the poor and shunned by independent laborers such as skilled artisans. In France, state subsidized protofactories gathered workers together in a similar fashion to produce luxury goods for the king's court. Americans were appalled by these scenes of impoverished, dependent masses forced into manufacturing luxury goods for aristocrats. Even more appalling, the conditions arose not only from natural population pressure, but also from deliberate government policy.[45]

Even so, with rapid population growth and periodic bouts of agricultural surpluses and unemployment in America, proposals to promote manufacturing employment for the idle poor surfaced during every commercial crisis. Agrarian republicanism notwithstanding, no matter how cheap land was there were always those unemployed who had neither the skills, capital nor desire to begin a farm. Back in the 1780s the problem of urban poverty was already pressing, and cities of high poverty and population density such as Boston, New York, and Philadelphia were subsidizing houses of manufacture to lighten the public relief burden.[46] The advocates of this policy, needing to offset the fear that growing numbers of factory workers would remain dependent paupers unfit for a republican society, eventually attempted to define them as members of the respectable "producing classes." They claimed that American workers were distinguished from European by being better paid, housed, and educated. High wages, or owning a house or a savings account, were characterized as forms of property giving a degree of economic independence and evidencing the honored traits of initiative, thrift, foresight, and attachment to the community.[47]

However, the generalized prejudice against wage laborers as part of the class of the urban poor was not to be overcome quickly (the mid-century Irish immigrants filling these classes added fuel to the fire), even though the steady mechanization of production continually added former artisans, household craft workers, and farmers to the ranks of those working for someone else. As this employment was largely low paying, irregular and periodically depressed, naturally wage labor and poverty were close cousins.[48] Eventually any form of voluntary private employment would be enough to detach someone from the stigma of dependency, but early efforts to move opinion in this direction most likely only reinforced the stigma on the unemployed; those poor who had no work at all had no one arguing on behalf of their republican character traits. In the feverish economic development of the mid-nineteenth century a preoccupation with gainful work was beginning to become a noticeable American characteristic.[49] As it seemed opportunities to get ahead were everywhere and everyone was trying to take advantage of them, the unemployed poor were all the more likely to be looked down on as people of defective character. New reformers turned their attention to this old problem, and advocated a more advanced method to discipline such people.

The method, paralleling the growth of factory manufacturing, was institutionalization. Publicly supported specialized institutions were promoted as instruments for the reformation of character. This was the time when public schools, penitentiaries, reformatories, and insane asylums were proliferating as replacements for the waning power of local communities to exert social control over their dependent and deviant members.[50] The Poor Law system had not changed very significantly since the colonial days (the western territories copied the poor laws of the eastern states), and in the large cities the cost of public relief was becoming increasingly onerous. State commissions, following the lead of private bodies, investigated conditions and identified a principle problem as indiscriminate giving due to the difficulty of clearly distinguishing the impotent from the able-bodied poor. One of the first of these reports laid out fears which were widely shared:

> The poor begin to consider it as a right; next, they calculate upon it as an income. The stimulus to industry and economy is annihilated or weakened, temptations to extravagance and dissipation are increased in proportion as public supply is likely or certain or desirable. The just pride of independence so honorable to man in every condition is thus corrupted by the certainty of public provision, and is either weakened or destroyed according to the facility of its attainment or its amount.[51]

The dependency of the poor, in accord with the republican tradition, was presented not merely an economic condition, but as a source of moral and social corruption. The reformers saw the growth of public relief as a cause of increased dependency, and recommended replacement of all forms of "outdoor relief" (aid given outside of institutions) with almshouses and workhouses. Institutionalized custody was expected to discourage applications for relief, scare the able-bodied into finding employment, save money, and make the supervision of forced labor easier.[52] The long area-by-area crusade for the reform of public relief lasted throughout the century and came to a climax in its last decades, when ten of the nation's largest cities eliminated, and many others reduced, outdoor relief to the poor.[53]

5. THE POSITIVE PROGRAM: FREE LAND FOR THE POOR

Still, the aim of salvaging some of the poor by turning them into independent farmers had not died during this time, and in fact took on a new life. Horace Greeley, a newspaper editor who was to become a national political figure, witnessed the impoverishment and extreme privations of citizens in New York City following the Panic of 1837 and took to encouraging surplus laborers in the cities to "go West." Leaders of nascent labor organizations, believing westward emigration would improve wages and working conditions for those who stayed behind, had begun agitating to make small plots of the public lands available to settlers at a nominal price—in effect, a free homestead. Eventually Greeley joined the movement and helped bring it to national attention. By the early 1850s, several homestead bills had received serious attention in Congress, although they failed to get through the Senate.[54]

The homestead movement was the climax of the long struggle to place the public lands in the hands of actual settlers, and although the congressional debates were primarily dominated by the goal of national economic development, they were also clearly marked with the language of agrarian republicanism. The effects of land monopolies in ancient Rome, feudal Europe and contemporary Ireland were contrasted with the republican institutions supported by widespread property ownership in America, and the growing numbers of wage workers and paupers in American cities were presented as danger signs of the machinations of "aristocratic" land speculators and industrial "barons." All participants saw development of the public lands as the key to economic growth, but homesteading advocates claimed that such settlement was necessary to maintain the underpinnings of republicanism via access to land for the poor.[55]

> Then, who is it that should not support this measure of HOMES FOR ALL? Look at its wooing incentives to industry, frugality, temperance, independence, love of country, virtue, and adoration to the beneficent donor—the Father of all. . . . Turn out all your "loose (not tied) floating population" upon the wild lands, and soon they will become virtuous, independent, and a bulwark to the country . . . and while you complain of poor taxes and almshouses—of jails and penitentiaries—you contribute greatly to the number of inmates by usurping their rights, and by denying to them the very means of life . . .[56]

> Let each man have a home, and when your elections come around he is a freeman, he is an independent man; he goes to the ballot-box and votes his own vote, and not the vote of his landlord or his master. Build up these districts, and there you will have virtue; there you will have honesty in private as well as public affairs, for after all, the people of the rural districts are to be trusted. . . . They do not live by politics, but they live by their labor, and they want the best government, the purest government that they can get. Go there amidst your rural population; there is industry, there is virtue, and intelligence . . .[57]

However, in the political climate of the later 1850s homesteading became a sectional issue between North and South; settlement of the west by free laborers was seen as a device to block the extension of slavery.[58] The homestead movement was tapped by a new Republican Party, whose rhetoric centered on the concept of "free labor": the idealization of social mobility in the dynamic economy of the North, in which through hard work, thrift and the other traditional virtues anyone could advance to independent self-employment with a farm, business, or shop of one's own. Southern society was regarded as the antithesis of this ideal, where the character of blacks was stunted by slavery and poor whites lost their respect for manual labor. For the Republicans, the tradition of the virtuous independent property owner included the whole class of small entrepreneurs, and entrepreneurial opportunity was what kept wage workers from being degraded into permanent dependency.[59]

In face of the widespread unemployment following the Panic of 1857, while many Republicans still blamed the poor as improvident, lazy, and dependent, there was a growing recognition that people suffered because jobs were scarce and wages low. As public charity was thought to increase dependency, the homestead act reemerged as a way to transform the dependent urban poor into good independent citizens by enticing them into migrating west.[60] In 1859 and 1860 Congressional Republicans fought hard to get a homestead act past southern opposition, only to see it vetoed by President Buchanan. But with the electoral victory of Lincoln and its aftermath of southern secession, the Republicans had a free field and reenacted the bill. President Lincoln signed the act on May 20, 1862.[61] Horace Greeley exulted over

> . . . one of the most beneficent and vital reforms ever attempted in any age or clime—a reform calculated to diminish sensibly the number of paupers and idlers and increase the proportion of working, independent, self-subsisting farmers in the land evermore.[62]

As it had special meaning for a very significant subgroup of the poor, the next of the several subsequent homesteading laws is also worth mentioning. Immediately following the war, radical Republicans proposed to confiscate some southern properties to make more homesteads available to ex-slaves as well as to poor whites. Their chief aim was the destruction of the southern "aristocracy" and movement towards the ideal of widespread small property ownership. Moderates blocked these efforts, but in 1866 Congress passed a bill ordering that the remaining public lands in the southern states be offered for homesteading only, without restrictions based on race or color, and temporarily barred to those who had borne arms against the Union. It was the first time any public lands were restricted exclusively to homesteaders, and the first American legislation to bar discrimination based on race. However, for a variety of reasons the act was disappointing in its implementation and within ten years was repealed.[63]

6. CONCLUSION: A LEGACY
OF POLITICAL LANGUAGE

The practical legacy of the early homesteading acts was mixed. By 1862 most of the best land had long since been taken; about two-thirds of the approximately one billion acres of remaining federal land were not suitable for farming.[64] Over the next twenty years there were about a half-million homesteading entries begun (representing over fifty million acres), but little more than a third of these were completed. A great many of these claims were filed by "dummies" on behalf of business interests who stripped the lands of their timber or mineral resources and then abandoned them; claims were also abandoned when settlers found their land to be unproductive or experienced other problems.[65] Furthermore, despite the ostensible policy of dedicating the remaining public lands to actual settlers, Congress added around a hundred million acres to those already granted to the railroads.[66]

All in all, the continued use of the rhetoric of agrarian republicanism obscured the declining availability of unsettled arable land and the transition from an agricultural to an industrial economy. Advances in the technology of agriculture were making it more and more difficult for small freeholders to survive; the 1880 census revealed that farm tenancy and indebtedness were growing, as were huge mechanized farm sized landholdings.[67] Most of the homesteaders were eastern farmers moving west, not the poor and working classes escaping the cities. Already by 1860 about half the labor force was employed for wages; from 1860 to 1890 the total population doubled, while the number employed by manufacturing more than tripled. The American search for new opportunities was characterized by rural to urban migration rather than urban to rural.[68]

Clearly the material conditions which gave rise to the ethical tradition of agrarian republicanism were disappearing, and many of its political functions—promoting agricultural over manufacturing interests, bringing the public lands more quickly to market, speeding the settlement of the West—were becoming battles of the past. One would expect it to have soon become useless as a means of creating meaning for political actors. Although homesteading retained its political popularity well into the early twentieth century, the widespread failures of settlers on the arid lands of the far west under the homesteading acts of 1909 and 1916 culminated in a shift of federal policy from homesteading to public management of the remaining public lands.[69] Despite all this, the agrarian republican tradition, centered on the idea that owning and working one's own land developed the moral and civic virtues, persisted into the new century.

For one thing, its tenets were deliberately perpetuated by politicians and civic leaders attempting to forestall the migration from rural to urban areas. "Back to the land" movements arose glorifying the virtues of the farming life whenever the business cycle was down and urban unemployment was up, even as late as the onset of the Great Depression. For example, the somewhat skeptical governor of New York, Franklin D. Roosevelt, experimented with using state relief money to place unemployed families on subsistence farms.[70] This reappeared in his presidency as the Subsistence Homesteading program of the early New Deal. The idea was for former farmers among the urban unemployed to be resettled, not on the frontier, but on farms held by insurance and mortgage companies, where they could feed themselves and supposedly buy these properties through working the land. As was soon pointed out, this flew in the face of the fact that farm incomes were so depressed that cash-crop farmers had been going bankrupt all over the country. The plan thus shifted from resettling the urban unemployed on repossessed farms to building utopian agricultural-industrial communities, but eventually ended up as government-subsidized suburban housing tracts.[71]

The survival of the agrarian republican tradition can be seen even more clearly in the enactment of the Bankhead-Jones Farm Tenant Act of 1937. The original legislation proposed to market bonds, buy land with the proceeds, and resell the land on very favorable terms to impoverished tenant farming families. Central to the promotion of the bill, the details of which were modified during the course of congressional consideration, was the appeal to the traditional ideal of the landowning citizen-farmer:[72]

> In all our plans we are guided, and will continue to be guided, by the fundamental belief that the American farmer, living on his own land, remains our ideal of self-reliance and of spiritual balance—the source from which the reservoirs of the Nation's strength are constantly renewed. . . . We want to perpetuate that ideal . . . under modern conditions, so that man may be strong in the ancient virtues . . . (Franklin D. Roosevelt)[73]

Both the subsistence homesteading and the tenant-ownership programs ended up in the Farm Security Administration (FSA), which was later destroyed by its political opponents. These opponents also relied on the traditional ideal of owner-occupied farms in their rhetoric, such as in their argument that the FSA was promoting collectivized farming, or that it was keeping its clients dependent by continuing to hold title to resettled lands for unnecessarily long periods of time.[74]

But it is not surprising that the language of agrarian republicanism lived on in agricultural policy debates; what is surprising is its presence in other areas of policy. That presence is the subject of the next few chapters.

Chapter 3

Homeownership for the Poor

The post-Civil War homesteading acts could have been the swan song of agrarian republicanism, an ethical tradition doomed to wane along with the dominance of farming in the U.S. economy. However, at least one way it survived outside of agricultural policy was by being adapted to the promotion of homeownership. The association of private homeownership with the traditional republican virtues originally linked to land ownership appeared in poverty policy in two ways. First, the language has been used to oppose public housing programs. Second, it has also been used to promote homeownership programs aimed at the poor. In this chapter, I trace the transfer of agrarian republicanism to homeownership policies and focus on its use in promoting homeownership for the poor. I conclude by identifying a key problem in the coherence of the ethical tradition as so adapted.

1. From Agrarian Republicanism to the Homeownership Ethic

The eclipse of the agricultural era by the industrial era heralded not the demise, but the transformation of agrarian republicanism. Just as FDR's Subsistence Homesteading program had evolved into subsidized housing tracts,[1] agrarian republicanism evolved into an ethic of homeownership. As

43

a sign of the status of free citizenship and a symbol of the virtues of industry, thrift, commitment to the community, and to political stability, homeownership since colonial times had performed many of the same symbolic
functions as the ownership of productive land.[2] What changed in the twentieth century was that the relative importance of farm ownership in per-
forming these symbolic functions was rapidly diminishing, while that of
homeownership was rising. "The family farm" as a repository of traditional
virtues may still be familiar, but farmers have come to represent only a small
sector of the population, while homeowners have gradually overtaken them
as the metaphorical "backbone of the nation."

The organization of the real estate profession at the end of the nineteenth century gave institutionalized support to the idealization of homeownership, as in these words before a professional convention: "Let me
tell you that the good home is the unit of good government. . . . There is
nothing more important to the public than that the people of the United
States should own their home, own the soil where they live."[3] By 1919
this theme was being shared by the federal government, as the National
Association of Real Estate Boards (NAREB) worked with the U.S.
Department of Labor on its national "Own Your Own Home" campaign
aimed at stimulating construction employment, and began promoting
national legislation to assist in mortgage financing.[4]

The onset of the Great Depression provided their opportunity, as
nearly one-third of unemployed laborers were from the building trades,[5]
and the widespread inability of homeowners to meet their mortgage payments was as serious a problem as the inability of farmers to meet theirs.
President Hoover's 1931 Conference on Home Building and Home
Ownership, which was dominated by banking and construction interests,
used agrarian republican language to call for government action: "Nothing creates greater stability in government than a wide distribution of
property ownership on the part of the people interested in that government." They went on to say that democracy is not possible "where tenants overwhelmingly outnumber home owners."[6] (Jefferson would have
said, "where tenants and dependent laborers outnumber landowners," but
by this time dependent laborers did outnumber independent farmers.)
Hoover addressed the conference in similar terms:

> . . . every one of you here is impelled by the high ideal
> and aspiration that each family may pass their days in the
> home which they own. . . . This aspiration penetrates the

heart of our national well-being. It makes for happier married life, . . . it makes for better citizenship. There can be no fear for a democracy or self-government or for liberty or freedom from homeowners no matter how humble they may be. . . . To own one's own home is a physical expression of individualism, of enterprise, of independence, and of the freedom of spirit.[7]

The ultimate results of these efforts were the Federal Home Loan Bank Act of 1932 and, under Roosevelt, the Home Owners' Loan Act of 1933 and the Federal Housing Act of 1934, acts which aimed at assisting the financing, refinancing, and insuring of home mortgages. With the deepening of the depression, the policy debates surrounding these acts tended to focus on the goal of stimulating employment and the details of the programs rather than idealizing homeownership. But in implementing the policies the Federal Housing Administration (FHA) revitalized the Own Your Own Home campaign carried on earlier by the U.S. Labor Department.[8] Promoting homeownership and maintaining employment for the masses now went hand in hand, offering at least an indirect link between homeownership and economic growth in place of the former direct link between frontier homesteading and economic development.

The federal role in promoting homeownership through regulatory, insurance, and tax measures has come to benefit a wide spectrum of supporters, including the middle classes who buy the homes, the construction industry which builds them, the realtors who sell them, and the credit institutions which finance them. Relatively few have opposed these policies, and even fewer have challenged the rhetoric surrounding them. Homeownership had historically wavered between 45–48 percent of the population, dropping slightly during the Great Depression, but from 1940 to 1980 it shot up to nearly 65 percent thanks to FHA and other federal programs, particularly income tax deductions.[9]

As homeownership rose in economic and political importance and took on the symbolic role previously assigned to land ownership, some policy entrepreneurs began to call for giving the poor an opportunity to attain this status, just as nineteenth-century reformers had called for making land more accessible to them. The idea was all the more compelling given that the main thrust of housing policy for the poor directly contradicted the homeownership ethic.

2. PUBLIC HOUSING AND ITS OPPONENTS

American legislation to regulate the housing conditions of the poor and eliminate slums goes back to the earliest colonial times, the primary concerns usually being that such an environment creates threats to public health and breeds an economic class antipathetic to property and republican virtues. Direct government provision of better housing, however, would have violated the prevailing view that the poor should work and save in order to escape the slums and own their own homes.[10]

Interest by the national government dates from the rapid growth of industrial urban neighborhoods at the turn of the century, with study commissions created for Congress in 1892 and for President Theodore Roosevelt in 1902. The Roosevelt commission did recommend, among other things, that the government purchase and improve tenements to rent or sell to the poor at affordable rates. Although government-owned housing for the working class was already established in Britain, this idea was ahead of its time in the United States, despite the national government's extensive experience in owning and operating housing for the military and for civilian employees at military installations. This experience did serve it during the housing shortage of World War I in providing private defense employees with affordable housing, most of which was sold following the war. That program in turn established the precedent for later actions in federal housing loans to limited dividend corporations and in direct federal construction of housing projects outside of the military; however, as in other social policy areas, it took the Great Depression to provoke federal involvement in housing the poor.[11]

In 1932, in the early stages of the depression and at the end of the Hoover administration, Congress authorized low-rent housing construction loans to limited-dividend corporations in an attempt to stimulate the housing industry, eliminate slums, and provide decent homes for low-income families. The following year, under Franklin Roosevelt's New Deal, this limited program was expanded and transferred to the new Public Works Administration. Within another year, the low number of eligible loan applications and high rents in completed projects led the PWA to change its focus to the direct construction and subsidization of housing projects, which they planned eventually would be managed by local authorities.[12] A 1935 proposal for legislation to put what was created as a temporary, emergency program on a permanent basis was stalled in Congress for two and a half years, until passage of the Housing Act of 1937.

This act ratified the federal role, built incrementally over half a decade, in subsidizing and guiding the construction and operation of public housing by local public housing authorities.

The New Deal gave us what are still some of the basic premises of our national housing policy: mortgage insurance and a secondary mortgage market for the middle class on the one hand, and public housing for the poor on the other. The former are compatible with the homeownership ethic, but the latter runs directly counter to it, and has been subject to controversy from the very start. The homeownership ideal was prominent in the NAREB-led opposition to public housing, which was particularly vehement in the decades after World War II. New funds for public housing (except for defense industry uses) had been suspended during the war because of the needs of war production. But after the war, a provision to construct more public housing in the Housing Act of 1949, a response to the postwar housing shortage which set a goal of "a decent home and a suitable living environment for every American family," was contested fiercely, barely surviving floor attempts in the House of Representatives to kill it. Even though it passed, the number of units actually funded was continually scaled back in subsequent appropriations decisions.[13]

Leonard Freedman, in his study of this opposition, blamed it largely on a "climate of ideas and attitudes" comprised of disdain for the poor, racial prejudice, and an ideology opposing government ownership in favor of the ideal of individual freedom through widespread property ownership—that is, owning one's own home.[14] Charges of socialism were pervasive. A typical statement by the opposition was: "Freedom and civilization depend upon the widespread ownership of property. . . . We must look to more home ownership as the principle means of attaining the maximum diffusion of property ownership."[15] While modern government-interventionist liberalism and the obvious failure of the private housing market to provide decent homes for the poor helped maintain a tenuous pro-public housing coalition, their legislative successes have only fleetingly occurred during galvanizing crises such as the Great Depression, a severe housing shortage, or urban riots.

By the 1960s many supporters had come to acknowledge defects in public housing programs, and many opponents realized that public housing was not about to become more than a minute component of the overall housing stock. Writing late in the decade, Freedman saw a "new, more pragmatic climate" producing three basic concepts at the heart of a variety of new proposals for housing the poor: a greater role for public-private partnership, large-scale rehabilitation of existing housing stock, and creating opportunities for the poor to own their own homes.[16] The concepts were not new, but they could gain attention only after the issue of public housing had ceased monopolizing the policy debates. Although the budget pressures of the Vietnam War and concerns about inflation caused difficulties for all housing programs at the end of the 1960s and into the 1970s, these "new" concepts were to persist into the 1980s as major housing issues.

3. Helping the Poor Buy Homes

Given the importance of the homeownership ethic and the concomitant animus against public housing, one could predict that proposals to help poor people become homeowners would eventually reach the national policy agenda. There have been two main approaches toward this end: (1) making credit more accessible to low-income homebuyers in the private housing market, which was tried on a fairly large scale from the late 1960s to the early 1970s, and (2) privatizing public housing, which was prominent on the political agendas of the Ronald Reagan and George Bush administrations. Programs of both types have drawn implicitly and explicitly from concepts associated with frontier homesteading and agrarian republicanism. This section reviews initiatives of the first type. The second approach is considered in the next two sections.

Federal programs directed specifically at poor rural residents have provided loans for homes as well as for farmland and farming needs from the 1930s up to the present.[17] There have also been programs to help low-income Native Americans on reservations to own their own homes.[18] But aside from these rural residents and some of the subsistence homesteaders mentioned earlier,[19] aid for homeownership was restricted to the middle (and upper) class until the 1960s. Then Section 221(d)(2) of the Housing Act of 1961 broke new ground by making federal insurance on long-term, low down payment mortgages available to those whose incomes were too high for public housing eligibility, but too low to afford to buy housing on ordinary terms.[20] This measure, the extension of a program for families displaced by government actions, came in response to the recognition that there was no longer the general backlog of demand for housing which characterized the postwar years, and that the slump in the housing industry would have to be addressed by targeting credit on families of modest means.[21]

Five years later, Section 221(h) of the Demonstration Cities and Met-ropolitan Development (Model Cities) Act provided mortgage insurance and technical assistance for nonprofit organizations buying and rehabili-tating substandard housing for resale to families in the same income cat-egory as public housing residents, and also provided insurance and subsidies for low-interest mortgages to the families.[22] This initiative, for which House Democrat Leonor Sullivan received unanimous bipartisan support in the housing subcommittee, was based on the experience of a private nonprofit organization in her St. Louis, Missouri, district.[23] As with the 1961 program, it was implemented on a modest, pilot-program scale. Then the outbreak of urban riots in 1967 opened the policy "win-dow" which was to result in new housing legislation, including the first large-scale low-income homeownership program.

Senator Charles Percy, a recently elected Illinois Republican who had made a campaign theme of homeownership for the poor as a pre-ventative against riots, advanced the most prominent proposal, also based on the St. Louis experience. "One Senator said he is going to call the bill 'the Urban-Rural Homestead Act of 1967,'" Percy stated. "If it works, the program should stimulate anew the spirit of self-help and self-reliance among individual families and get them moving up the lad-der."[24] The chief feature of his bill was the establishment of a National Home Ownership Foundation which would channel private and public funds to nonprofit organizations making long-term, low-interest mort-gage loans to low-income families. The federal government would sub-sidize the interest payments, and families who could not afford a down payment could substitute sweat equity (their own labor in finishing or improving the house). This was all meant to give them the opportunity "through their own effort, energy, willingness, determination, and per-severance to own their own home, to gain an economic stake in their own community, and to have the pride and self-esteem that comes with homeownership."[25]

Percy and his allies made claims for homeownership that harked back to the traditional arguments about land ownership:

> For a man who owns his own home acquires a new dignity. He begins to take pride in what is his own, and pride in con-serving and improving it for his children. He becomes a more steadfast and concerned citizen of his community. He becomes more self-confident and self-reliant. Becoming a

homeowner transforms him. It gives him roots, a sense of belonging, a true stake in his community and its well-being.[26]

. . . homeownership makes an individual a better citizen, as it gives him an added reason for showing more concern about the actions of his Government . . . these individuals will become contributing members of society, in contrast to the other methods now available which would make them more recipient than contributor.[27]

. . . opportunity for homeownership instills a sense of pride by allowing an individual a fair chance to earn something tangible which he can conserve for himself and for his family. It helps him plant the roots from which traditionally have flowered the sense of civic pride, family responsibility and individual dignity that have made our nation strong.[28]

Some of us have been greatly concerned about the growing incursions upon property rights of citizens. I believe that if more individuals owned property, there would be greater support, stronger support, and more profound support for the constitutional and natural rights of property in the country . . . that nation is safest in which people own their own homes, regardless of how humble their homes may be. This gives the property owner something to live for, something to work for, and something to die for. I do not know of anything more conducive to the future stability and security of our country than that objective which the distinguished Senator seeks to achieve—the ownership of his own property, his own little vine and fig tree, by the individual who is in the low-income or moderate-income bracket.[29]

The biblical image of the "vine and fig tree" was a little incongruent, since the owners were obviously not expected to farm their lands. Senator Brooke attempted to cool down the rhetoric with the reminder that "in order to obtain the anticipated results [the transformation into productive citizens able to repay the government for the federal subsidies], prospective homeowners will have to be employed, or employable at comparatively high wages."[30]

The objectives of the Percy bill, which was cosponsored by all the Republican senators, were long advocated by liberal housing organizations, and had wide political appeal even though Housing and Urban Development (HUD) Secretary Robert Weaver contended that poor families should not be burdened with the responsibilities of homeownership. In the subcommittee consideration John Sparkman, the Democratic chair of the Banking and Currency Committee and its Housing Subcommittee, eventually negotiated a unanimous compromise merging Percy's bill with one introduced by Democratic Senator Walter Mondale. The functions of the National Home Ownership Foundation were reduced to offering technical advice and some seed money to nonprofit organizations, with the bulk of the mortgage money for low-income homebuyers expected to come through private banks and the Federal Housing Administration. The primary benefit provided by the government would be interest subsidies.[31]

President Johnson's 1968 housing proposals responded to the congressional interest in homeownership for the poor, and he summarized the common refrain:

> Home ownership is a cherished dream and achievement of most Americans. But it has always been out of reach of the nation's low-income families. Owning a home can increase responsibility and stake out a man's place in his community. The man who owns a home has something to be proud of and good reason to protect and preserve it.[32]

Congressional action on the proposals, again against a backdrop of riots, including those in Washington following the assassination of Martin Luther King Jr., was relatively swift. Title I of the 1968 Housing and Urban Development Act established mortgage interest subsidies for low to moderately low-income families which could bring the effective interest rate down as low as 1 percent. Down payment requirements were also extremely low. The provision, usually referred to as Section 235, made an impact quickly: in 1970 about 30 percent of low-priced houses were purchased through Sec. 235, and by the end of that year the number of low-income housing units purchased through it was over one-tenth the number provided by the public housing program over the previous thirty years.[33]

But criticism of Sec. 235 soon arose over cases of FHA-insured mortgages on substandard quality homes with shoddy repair work. A 1971 study argued that most of the problems in FHA-insured houses were due, not to Sec. 235, but to another provision in the 1968 act which pushed the FHA to stop redlining inner city neighborhoods and caused a relaxation in the agency's appraisal standards. The study also complained that provisions for homeownership counseling to Sec. 235 buyers were not funded and consequently it was rarely done.[34] In any event, congressional hearings in 1972 made it clear that abuses in HUD urban programs were widespread, resulting in high default rates on government-insured mortgages, and it was Sec. 235s low-income homeownership program that attracted the most attention.[35] In January of 1973, President Nixon declared a moratorium on all subsidized housing and community development programs and impounded their funds. Following a formal reevaluation of housing and urban programs, the Housing and Community Development Act of 1974 replaced many categoric programs with block grants and moved the federal government away from housing supply subsidies towards increasing effective demand through rent supplements.

The act did include a revised and reduced Sec. 235; interest subsidies were lowered and down payment requirements raised in order to meet the criticism that the program was open to those too poor to bear the responsibilities of ownership. Congress didn't offer new funds for the program, but pressed for the release of previously appropriated but impounded funds, eventually resorting to legal action.[36] The executive branch resisted. HUD Secretary Carla A. Hill stated that "homeownership for the poor is probably an unrealistic goal in today's economy," arguing that the responsibilities of homeownership are too much for the poor. "When the plumbing backs up, when the heating acts up . . . these people do not have the wherewithal to deal with these problems." [37] Supporters of the program contended it was meant for modest-income families, not the poor, and blamed HUD administration for many of the problems. The administration finally agreed to the release of $264.1 million for Sec. 235,[38] and the program resumed in early 1976, aimed at a higher income group and limited to newly constructed homes. Activity was well below expectations, and continued at a low level despite liberalizations in the late 1970s.[39] Sec. 235 is currently inactive.

4. PRIVATIZING PUBLIC HOUSING: THE REAGAN YEARS

In 1957 the National Housing Conference, a private organization of influential housing activists, recommended that the design of public housing projects be "on a basis permitting their eventual sale to tenants either individually or on a cooperative basis."[40] A provision of the Housing Act of 1965 to allow public housing authorities to sell detached and semidetached housing units to tenants passed despite HUD Secretary Weaver's opposition.[41] Buyers would be able to use their monthly rental payments as a channel for accumulating a down payment. Its sponsor, Senator Tower of Texas, argued that "the existing practices in public housing tend to destroy the desire or interest of hundreds of thousands of families to participate in that great American privilege of property ownership—and property ownership is the greatest of all deterrents to communism."[42] The 1968 housing act extended the 1965 provisions to all units with sufficient individual identity to be appropriate for sale to their residents.[43] The option had not yet, however, been implemented by HUD. Ironically, the abandonment of homes under HUDs earlier program of homeownership for the poor was to contribute to the eventual launching of this second approach.

As the number of foreclosed or abandoned urban properties began to mount in the late 1960s and early 1970s, local initiatives in deeding properties to citizens who agreed to repair, occupy, and maintain such dwellings spread. The popular term "urban homesteading" made an analogy between investing sweat equity in abandoned urban properties and the pioneer development of the public lands. According to one author, much of the initial attention and support for the idea is traceable to the analogy, despite critics who pointed out the difference between the economic viability of 160 acres and "a shell of a dwelling with no real economic value."[44]

The 1974 housing act allowed HUD to supplement the local programs by turning over federally owned residential properties. Due to underfunding and the inherent difficulty of finding sufficiently attractive properties and competent homesteaders, implementation by HUD was never widespread, and despite later efforts to target the programs to lower-income households they have primarily benefited families who have access to resources for rehabilitation. But in the late 1970s HUD-funded demonstration projects, aimed at transferring to other cities New York's model of urban homesteading in multifamily complexes, showed that low-income cooperatives could be successful in reclaiming deteriorating buildings, although considerable technical assistance would be necessary and the risk of failure high.[45]

Multifamily properties abandoned by their owners were not always vacated; in some cases tenants stayed on and, out of necessity, learned to manage the properties. A similar strategy was used by public housing residents when authorities were unresponsive to bad conditions and tenant concerns. In a 1969 rent strike against the St. Louis Housing Authority, tenants took over buildings and eventually forced the Authority into bankruptcy. As part of the eventual settlement HUD gave the tenants' organization a continuing role in managing their homes. Based on the St. Louis example and at the urging of the Ford Foundation, HUD initiated a demonstration program in 1976 that showed that resident-management in public housing could be successful if subsidies were continued.[46] As any large-scale repairs required collateral for loans, resident ownership of the properties came to be seen by some as the next logical step.

Inspired by urban homesteading, public housing resident-management, and the British sell-off of 800,000 public housing units in the early 1980s, conservative policy analysts aligned with the Reagan administration began to champion the cause of privatizing public housing. (Other government assets and services had also been targeted for privatization.)[47] The President's Commission on Housing endorsed the sale of public housing to tenants as a policy option in its 1982 report.[48] By 1984 Representative Jack Kemp of New York had taken on a leading role, testifying at hearings on privatization before a subcommittee of the Joint Economic Committee and getting bills introduced in both houses of Congress. His proposed Urban Homestead Act of 1984 would have allowed the sale of public housing units to residents at 25 percent of market value, with no down payment, at interest rates no more than 70 percent of market rates for mortgages. The homesteading theme and the homeownership ethic pervaded his comments:

> Since the beginning of our country, tenantry has been viewed as unfavorable to freedom. The policy of free republics was always to multiply homeownership to increase the love of country, the spirit of independence, and self-reliance. Abraham Lincoln over a century ago endorsed a Homestead Act which opened up the Western frontier to the new immigrants and freed blacks seeking to own their own home. We name our bill in honor of Lincoln's Homestead Act since we share his objective of homeownership for all regardless of income, creed, or race.[49]

Homeownership is nearly synonymous with the American dream. Yet today, most urban poor find it nearly impossible to own a home. . . . We want to let these people know that their aspiration, their hopes, and their dreams are our own. That the American dream of homeownership is not just for the well-to-do, or the middle-class, but also for poor people who live in the most blighted areas of our inner cities. They too yearn for homeownership—a home in which to take pride while building and improving for the future and for their children.[50]

Kemp's bill died in committee, but the administration began action under existing laws. On October 23, 1984, HUD announced plans for a Public Housing Homeownership Demonstration program, and by June of the following year seventeen public housing authorities (PHAs) had been authorized to transfer a total of 1,290 units to tenants at affordable prices. The PHAs would select the units and set the price and terms of sale, while HUD would continue debt service on outstanding construction and rehabilitation bonds. Further rehabilitation costs and all operating expenses would be the buyer's responsibility. The first sale occurred to national publicity in 1986. By August of the following year 105 units were sold, 43 single-family and 62 multifamily units. HUD planned to sell at least another 1,600 units and, if the sales were successful, to further expand the program.[51]

The public housing privatization debate began in a highly partisan context, as throughout the 1980s a central housing issue had been the Republicans' renewed opposition to the construction of new public housing in favor of issuing rent vouchers to the poor. Periodically the Democrat-controlled House had attempted to pass new housing bills, but the Senate, with a Republican majority during Reagan's first six years, did not even hold hearings on the subject. Until 1987 the only housing authorization passed had barely made it through Congress as a rider to the 1983 authorization bill for the International Monetary Fund.[52] But resident ownership was to prove to have bipartisan appeal. Resident management had been instituted in the Kenilworth-Parkside public housing project in the District of Columbia, and the tenants now wanted to own their buildings. Thus, their congressional representative, Democrat Walter E. Fauntroy, joined with Kemp to revive his 1984 bill as an amendment to a 1986 housing bill. Kemp's coalition again called upon the imagery of frontier homesteading:

> We want to give folks an opportunity to repair, to pick up, to
> clean up, to refurbish, to do what was done in the nineteenth
> century when we had a homesteading act. This is, in my view,
> fitting into this whole concept of urban homesteading. We
> can provide opportunity for folks to have and to manage their
> own properties, their own housing, to give them a stake in
> that dream that all of us share irrespective of our color, culture,
> creed, or political philosophy.[53]

> It is radical the way the old homestead bill after the Civil War
> was radical. Back then we gave thousands of impoverished
> immigrants and Americans an opportunity they could hardly
> have imagined they would ever have, a chance to own their
> own piece of property on the frontier and to extend the
> boundaries of civilization westward. Like that breakthrough
> program, this amendment does much the same thing in
> America's inner cities.[54]

The familiar arguments about having a stake in one's community, about property inspiring pride, motivation, independence and so forth were reiterated. Democratic members of the housing subcommittee, however, raised concerns such as the shrinkage of the total public housing stock, the skimming off of the best units, and properties reaching the hands of speculators, arguments similar to those raised about the disposition of public lands through the original homesteading acts. They pressed Kemp to withdraw his amendment so that it might be more carefully drafted in committee hearings. Kemp was cautiously conciliatory, but other coalition members objected to the withdrawal and the amendment passed the Democratic House, 238–176.[55]

Although the housing bill also passed overwhelmingly in the House (419–1), it was blocked in the Senate. It was revived the following year, after the Republicans had lost eight Senate seats in the November election. The Democrats of the housing subcommittee had learned from the previous year's experience and added their own version of resident ownership, a demonstration program with significant restrictions (such as requiring that tenants later reselling their units must sell them back to the resident-management corporation and thus not use them for speculation and windfall profits). When a housing bill passed the Senate on March 31, the first time since Reagan had become President, the House activity speeded up. The housing bill reached the floor June 10, the chief issues being the overall cost of the bill and the Republicans' desire to issue more rental vouchers instead of constructing new public housing.[56]

During the floor debate, Kemp offered an Armey-Kemp Urban Homesteading amendment to alter the resident ownership provisions in line with the previous year's successful amendment.[57] It would revive the 25 percent of market value pricing and low-interest mortgages, limit resale restrictions to five years, and provide for the rehabilitation and sale of vacant public housing units. Unlike the previous year, it also offered some type of low-income housing program substitute for every unit sold. (This was a requirement that the House appropriations committee had placed on the administration's demonstration program.)[58] Opponents argued that the Kemp amendment offered a huge subsidy to a minority of the low-income population, and that the best units would wind up in the hands of speculators. Representative Morrison successfully offered a substitute amendment giving tenants a right to buy instead of making sales dependent on the permission of public housing authorities, but otherwise negating Kemp's more expansive program.

As finally passed, the 1987 Housing and Community Development Act reauthorized existing housing programs and added a few new ones, including the limited resident ownership program. It allowed HUD to sell public housing, at prices taking into account both fair market value and affordability, to qualified resident-management corporations (RMCs) who could then sell to residents. Public housing authorities could finance the sale if no other financing were available. HUD would continue to pay the debt service on bonds issued to build and modernize the units, but would not continue operating subsidies. Purchasers could only resell their homes back the RMC or to other eligible low-income families, and there were provisions for recapturing profits from resale within the first five years after the initial sale. Although there were replacement requirements for each unit sold, no financing for this was provided. As there were very few qualified RMCs in the country and the funding of the program was left uncertain, this was but a minor step towards resident ownership.[59]

5. Secretary Kemp's HOPE

It was the 1988 Presidential election that opened the way for a more ambitious program. On December 19 President-elect George Bush named Jack Kemp as the new secretary of HUD. At Congressional committee hearings before and after his confirmation by the Senate (100–0), Kemp extolled resident ownership of public housing, urban "enterprise zones," and other ideas promoting more widespread property ownership.[60]

> I would also like to have somebody think about how we could take a [rent] voucher or a certificate and have an element in there that would give people some equity, some chance of maybe using it as a potential for maybe a down payment someday if they made that decision. I think this word equity is a beautiful word. You want equity, i.e., fairness, you want equity in the system, and anything that gives people a sense of the dignity that comes with ownership or a piece of the pie, whether they are a worker that owns their business or has a stake in the company, whether they are public housing residents can have a piece of that public housing pie, anything we can do to give people a stake or an equity in the system.[61]

The effort to privatize public housing was gradually becoming tied to a broader argument about the importance of giving a property "stake" to lower-income citizens, in which homeownership was recognized as but one kind of asset.

Kemp took office in February, intending to push a major housing initiative, but in April the HUD inspector general disclosed influence peddling during the Reagan administration, setting off a major scandal and diverting Kemp's attention to the development of a HUD reform bill. In the meantime, he persuaded President Bush and Budget Director Richard Darman to support a $4 billion, three–year housing program, the first new Republican housing program in a decade, to be called Home Ownership and Opportunity for People Everywhere (HOPE), with various forms of resident ownership as the centerpiece.[62]

That fall committees in both houses were moving on major housing bills. In October, congressional Democrats threatened to tie passage of the HUD reform bill to a reauthorization of housing policy, although Kemp said he would not be ready for reauthorizations until early in the next year. Bush was forced to act by the Democrats' strategy and in November announced Kemp's HOPE initiatives.[63] On this evidence of the administration's intention to pass new housing legislation, the bills were decoupled and the reform bill passed on the brink of adjournment. The starting point for the housing reauthorization bill the next year would be three dramatically different proposals: the House bill, the Senate bill, and Kemp's HOPE program.[64]

In March of the following year Kemp officially presented HOPE before congressional housing subcommittees. Provisions included grants for residents purchasing public housing properties; grants to help low-income people purchase vacant HUD-held multifamily projects and single-family homes; obligating owners prepaying mortgages on federally subsidized low-income rental units to give tenants a right of first refusal to purchase buildings with HUD grants; requiring public housing agencies to develop local programs to help families become economically independent; and allowing the secretary of HUD to designate fifty Housing Opportunity Zones opposing restrictive zoning codes and other obstacles to affordable housing. To gain support, Kemp included the requirement that public housing units sold to their residents could only be resold back to the RMC, at a price limited to the cost of the down payment and any improvements, plus inflation.[65]

Over the next two months the subcommittees worked on the housing bills, and by June a housing bill had reached the floor of the Senate. The heart of the bill was a new grant program: HOP, Housing Opportunity Partnership (later to become HOME Investment Partnerships), offering money to cities and states to rehabilitate low-income housing units. Kemp wanted some HOP funds for HOPE. The Democrats liked HOPE, but believed it failed to meet the need for new low-income housing; they offered what Kemp considered to be only token funding. Negotiations bogged down on June 18, but a veto threat got them moving again. Finally an agreement was reached, with Kemp getting HOPE fully funded.[66] The bill passed the Senate, 96 to 1.

In the meantime Kemp, soon to become the head of President Bush's new Economic Empowerment Task Force, began pushing a "national agenda to help low-income people."[67] In an interview in *The New Republic*, Kemp argued that the "challenge is to convince people on the left, right, and center that something can be done to give people a chance to have assets, and property, and capital, and education." He wanted to see a million public housing tenants become owners, arguing that government has a role to play in getting poor people out of dependency and into the economic and social mainstream.[68]

On August 1, the House of Representatives passed a housing bill with a HOPE provision similar to the Senate's. Although conference negotiations got tied up in a squabble over revamping the Federal Housing Administration, by the end of October a conference report was adopted by both houses authorizing the programs for the new fiscal year which had begun on October 1. On November 11 President Bush signed the Cranston-Gonzalez National Affordable Housing Act, singling out the HOPE provisions:

> Now, let me start with a story, a bit of history—1862, the middle of the Civil War. And on May 20th of that year, Abraham Lincoln sat down with pen in hand and signed into law the Homestead Act of 1862. And that bill gave 160 acres to any family who wanted to make a go of it in the wilderness and reach for the American dream.
>
> It is one of the most successful endeavors in American history, causing the great land rush to the Wild West and forming the vision for a new homesteading program in urban America today. Because Abraham Lincoln's Homestead Act empowered people, it freed them to control their own destinies, to create their own opportunities, and to live the vision of the American dream. Likewise today, creating the opportunity for low-income Americans to become property owners is a key to fighting poverty and offering real hope to thousands . . . HOPE will provide new opportunities for low-income families to buy their own homes—urban homesteaders, if you will—and helps the residents of public housing to buy their own units.[69]

However, appropriations decisions had already been made and contained no money for the new programs. In February, Kemp sought to divert money from old housing programs to his newly authorized ones, but the appropriations subcommittees blocked him.[70] For the coming fiscal year, House appropriators recommended $210 million of Kemp's requested $865 million for his HOPE program, with no money for the public housing component. When the appropriations bill reached the floor, Mike Espy, a black Democrat from Mississippi interested in how Kemp's ideas could help his many low-income constituents, and Jim Kolbe, a longtime Kemp ally, offered an amendment to shift $151 million from "flexible subsidy" housing programs (grants / loans to developers to improve low-income rental housing) to HOPE I, the public housing title. Appropriations for these programs had exceeded authorizations by that amount.[71] Beyond the usual arguments repeated in the debates over the last several years, Espy's remarks in particular pointed to the importance of assets in a broader sense than just homeownership:

> Without accumulating assets, the poor are destined to remain poor. Assets, Mr. Chairman, not necessarily income, is what separates the haves from the have-nots. The richest 5 percent of Americans receive the same amount of income as the bottom 40 percent, but the richest 1 percent of Americans own more assets than the bottom 80 percent combined.[72]

Sixty-six Democrats and all of the Republicans voted to overrule the Appropriations Committee, 216 to 183. The following month Senate appropriations gave $440 million for HOPE, with $175 million for the public housing component.[73] Conferees gave $361 million for the HOPE programs. Kemp was not completely satisfied, but President Bush rejected his recommendation of a veto.[74]

The 1990 National Affordable Housing Act emphasized new obligations placed on recipients of housing aid (to look for jobs, stay in school, and so forth), better coordination of services, and the accumulation of assets. In addition to the HOPE provisions, it created a program that puts part of public housing rental payments in escrow to be given back to tenants if they get off government aid. During the rest of his tenure, Secretary Kemp pushed HUD to train large numbers of public housing residents to form resident management corporations and to prepare to become owners of their buildings. He also continued his efforts to promote a broadened antipoverty agenda based on ideas of "empowerment" and property ownership, such as in his proposed "Family Sufficiency Program," which would apply these principles to welfare and food stamp programs.[75] Although we shall see in chapter 5 that other proposals to help poor people acquire assets have been attractive to the Clinton administration, Kemp's HOPE program was not. With political attention focussed on the federal budget deficit, President Clinton raided the HOPE budget during his first year in office and slashed it further over the next two years, limiting funding to the very few sales of public housing units to tenants already planned when he came into office.[76]

6. Conclusion: Poverty and the Homeownership Ethic

To conclude this chapter, I would like to look a little more closely at the homeownership ethic as applied to the poor, and to identify a key problem which has bearing on the failure of the programs offered to realize its ideals.

The role of an updated version of agrarian republicanism is apparent in the policy history of homeownership for the poor. A recognizable set of symbols occurs repeatedly in the policy debates, the most obvious of which are the "homesteading" label and other references to the homesteading acts. The words "dependence" and "independence" are common, as are tropes such as having a "stake" in the community and using the term "the American dream" to refer to the successful acquisition of property. Negative symbols refer to life in public housing as "serfdom" or "living on the plantation"; the serf economies of Europe and the plantation slave economy were the antitheses of the ideal of a nation of yeoman farmers. Alternatively, the same disapproval of economic dependence is updated by comparing public housing to "socialized housing" or "housing in Russia." If the arguments are assembled into thematic groupings, no creativity is necessary to develop them into a clear and interrelated set of principles. They mirror the central tenets of agrarian republicanism:

1. Political freedom and the virtues that support it are of overarching importance. It is the economic independence of citizens that insures political freedom, by allowing them to exercise independent political judgment and choice. Economic independence is achieved through hard work and thrift aimed at the acquisition and improvement of property. Economic dependency leads to political despotism by eroding initiative, self-esteem, human dignity, and resistance to the spirit of servility in general. Ownership of property, on the other hand, inspires initiative, self-esteem and so on.

2. Freedom is not antithetical to social ties; citizens should commit themselves to caring for the well-being of others. Ownership of a piece of land with a home is a vehicle for commitments to family life and to involvement in local affairs. Patriotism and community pride

are the result of having a material "stake" in a society. The experience of property ownership also makes possible the respect for the natural right of property which is basic to the social contract.

3. Social equality demands that all citizens, regardless of the economic circumstances they are born into, have an opportunity to realize these ideals of citizenship if they are willing to work towards them. Devotion to the ideals must be rewarded by social status and economic security if they are to be successfully propagated. The government has the responsibility to use public resources to make such opportunities more widely available to those, currently poor, who are willing to take advantage of them.

In the various debates and public statements concerning the major programs for homeownership for the poor these principles have been referred to again and again. The opponents of the programs typically do not dispute the principles, but focus on the deficiencies of particular policy proposals for realizing the ideals. They argue that making property too accessible brings it into the hands of those who have not made themselves worthy of ownership, or into the hands of speculators; that the public resources being distributed are being used up without replenishment; or that programs will not reach enough people or haven't been tested yet. The one opposing argument that goes beyond the premises of the homeownership ethic is that the government has a responsibility for those who, for one reason or another, are incapable of achieving responsible property ownership, and that merely making property available should not be an excuse for avoiding this responsibility.

The most common opposition argument, which I have alluded to from time to time in my account, is closely related to this. It finds homeownership itself a deficient instrument for realizing the first of the above-specified principles. Simply stated, owning a home does not make one economically independent; in fact, it gives one an added economic responsibility, not the means to meet one's responsibilities. What the poor really need are good jobs. This argument runs throughout the policy history, but some of the most pointed examples come from the 1990 debate over the Kolbe-Espy amendment:

A recent report issued by the Budget Committee of this House indicates that the average income of public housing residents is less than $600 a month and the monthly operating costs of home ownership would exceed $300 a month. What family planner or economist envisions poor people spending 50 percent of their meager incomes for a mortgage and at the same time breaking the cycle of poverty?[77]

If you want to empower these people, let us talk about jobs, let us talk about job training, let us talk about education. Let us not talk about a silly idea of owning a unit that nobody wants to live in. . . . If they can get a job, they can be empowered. Let me tell you something, they will buy their home, and it will not be in a housing project; it will be in suburbia, or maybe next door to you.[78]

The people who live in public housing do not want to live there and certainly do not want to buy there. The people who live in public housing live there because they cannot afford to live anywhere else. . . . If we really want to help these people, defeat this amendment and give these people a chance to do what other Americans do: That is, buy a decent home in a decent neighborhood as a result of earning decent wages on a decent job.[79]

The homeownership ethic does not cohere in the way agrarian republicanism did. If economic independence is a key link in the chain of ideas, homeownership weakens it. There is something homeownership cannot give that farmland ownership, at least theoretically, could: an opportunity for the poor to work to support themselves. Working the land can produce an income, or at least some of the goods necessary for life. Owning your home, on the other hand, may provide an opportunity to invest labor in improvements for possible future capital gains, but it does not provide an income. (Unless one takes in boarders, but earning income as a landlord hardly fits the tradition.)

The promoters of programs for homeownership for the poor acknowledged job training and similar programs as important supplements to their proposals, although often the rhetoric made it sound as if owning a home in and of itself was the key to overcoming poverty. Their opponents saw that jobs are not supplementary, but primary to any economic "independence" for most citizens today. It has, of course, been a much more common policy proposal in the United States of the twentieth century to try to make jobs more accessible to the poor. Arguments about getting poor people off welfare programs and into jobs are the subject of the next chapter.

Chapter 4

Welfare and Work

In laying emphasis on preventing dependency over maintaining adequate incomes, U.S. poverty policy has continued to reflect the civic republican tradition throughout the twentieth century. Although a new liberal coalition struggled to institute income support for the poor, their proposals have been subject to repeated attacks associating such support with dependency, the demoralization of recipients, and the corruption of government, dooming the proposals to perpetual controversy and limited political appeal. But as land ownership had come to be replaced by employment as the foundation of economic independence, finding a policy to provide opportunities for poor citizens to become independent became problematic. The closest match to the model of nineteenth-century public land policies has been job training programs, which the government can parcel out to the poor in the hope that they will thereafter be able to make it on their own. Mandatory training or work experience programs have also been popular, and fit the long tradition of disciplining the behavior of the poor. Employment policies to insure that there are jobs available for all citizens, however, have been much more difficult to fit to the republican tradition.

1. Public Relief and the Fear of Corruption

Despite massive changes in the U.S. economy during the decades following the Civil War, the poor law system of public relief survived relatively unscathed. Funding and administration remained local, varying from place to place, and the association of dependence on public relief with moral and social corruption persisted; as late as 1934 fourteen states still barred recipients of public relief from voting or holding office.[1] Wage labor became less and less associated with dependency as it overtook independent farming and other forms of self-employment as the predominant occupational status, without too much worry over how this altered the traditional concept of economic independence. However, industrialization, with its low wages, cyclical depressions, technological displacements and industrial accidents, fed the growth of urban poverty, and this as always attracted anxious attention. But concerned citizens still predominantly blamed public relief for increasing dependence and sought ways to reform the character of the poor.

By the late nineteenth century faith in the reforming capacity of the ubiquitous poorhouse had been largely discredited, and, fearful of its abuse by malingerers despite abhorrent conditions which would seem sufficient deterrence, reformers undertook to purge poorhouses of able-bodied men.[2] As for outdoor relief, the "corruption" of political patronage associated with its distribution provoked the movement that abolished it in several major cities near the end of the century.[3] Even the defenders of outdoor relief (primarily its administrators) concurred that such relief tended to demoralize the poor, but argued that without it some people would starve. Where it survived, outdoor relief was structured to discipline and deter the able-bodied: onerous work was required in return for aid which was deliberately less than the wages of the lowest paid laborers (the principle of "less eligibility").[4] Reformers turned their hopes to private charity organizations, which were pioneering the method of systematic casework. Careful investigation of applicants took over the task of distinguishing the worthy from the unworthy poor in order to deal with each appropriately. For the able-bodied, this usually meant removal from relief and counseling to guide them into the virtuous habits thought to lead to independence.[5]

However, the depression of 1893–94 exposed the inadequacy of private relief and provoked new public efforts which carried into the early decades of the new century.[6] As part of a broader urban reform movement, newly named municipal offices of "public welfare" began to professionalize administration and adopted the casework method.[7] Cities experimented with temporary public works programs.[8] State boards of charity, originally set up to supervise institutions for special categories of the worthy poor such as the blind and the insane, began to monitor local general relief programs, although there was as yet negligible state funding or control.[9] Some advocates of more radical innovations, particularly people associated with the newly emerging social sciences, blamed increased poverty on economic causes rather than the moral corruption of the poor, but in political forums the traditional conceptions still prevailed. The only "scientific" viewpoint drawing wide support was found in the eugenics movement, which traced dependency to heredity and fed on prejudices about the character of southern and eastern European ethnics and African-Americans.[10]

The traditional republican conceptions were particularly prominent in the opposition to state pensions for aged workers. Impressed by European programs, reformers attempted to build on the American precedent of a huge national pension program for Civil War veterans and their survivors. This tactic backfired: the special pleading of veterans' organizations and the party patronage involved in the continual enlargements of these pensions brought to mind for many people the old association of outdoor relief with moral and political corruption. Middle- and upper-class fears of such corruption frustrated the hopes for a European-style reformist coalition throughout the critical decade of the 1910s.[11] Rhetoric about governments' lust for power and the importance of independent citizens, now tied to opposition to socialism, also helped squelch efforts for government-provided health and unemployment insurance.[12]

One reformist proposal that did overcome this opposition and become law in most of the states was aid to poor mothers with dependent children. Intervention into the upbringing of poor children had long been viewed as a key to ending the "cycle of dependency," but disillusionment with the institutionalization of children led to proposals to give poor single mothers stipends which would enable them to keep their children and stay home to care for them rather than take jobs outside the home. Opponents again linked such cash aid to outdoor relief and Civil War pensions as negative symbols invoking fears of demoralization and corruption, but vigorous networks of women's groups effectively countered with widely accepted ideas about protecting woman's proper sphere as homemaker and mother. Even so, although "aid to dependent children" programs spread rapidly after 1911 (the original "mothers' pensions" label was dropped because it signaled cash aid to able-bodied adults), most were carefully restricted to "morally fit" mothers, primarily white widows, who would be scrutinized for signs of moral corruption.[13]

When state pensions for the aged finally began to be established in the 1920s, they were also commonly restricted to the morally fit. Both types of programs, left largely to the discretion of local authorities, were often victims of underfunding and non-implementation.[14] Cash aid to the poor was unpopular not just because it was a tax burden and could interfere with labor markets, but because inherited political language threatened that it would be an ever-expanding source of moral corrosion. As a result, up through the 1920s the primary method of caring for the poor continued to be the local poorhouse.[15]

2. THE RIGHT TO WORK *VS.* THE DOLE

With rapid economic growth following the recession of the early 1920s, the momentum of social reform was lost in the belief that prosperity would soon overtake and abolish the existence of poverty in the United States. Emphasis returned to casework aimed at reforming the dependent, now with the aid of a corps of professionally trained social workers.[16] This optimism crashed along with the stock market in October 1929, at the beginning of the Great Depression. As economic distress dragged on year after year, private relief agencies and local governments were overwhelmed and resistance to state and even national government intervention gradually eroded. There were efforts to speed up public works projects to absorb some of the unemployment, but no significant state actions were taken until New York set up a Temporary Emergency Relief Administration (TERA) in September of 1931, two years after the crash. Public works spending was also increased by the national government, but President Hoover strongly resisted federal involvement in relief (although eventually he acceded to loans to the states for their relief programs):[17]

> I am opposed to any direct or indirect Government dole. . . .
> It is the duty of the National Government to insist that both
> the local governments and the individual shall assume and
> bear these responsibilities as a fundamental of preserving the
> very basis of our freedom.[18]

Hoover referred to federal relief as an "opiate" or a "dole." The latter term came from England's post-World War I unemployment benefits programs, which had succumbed to political pressures for expansion just as the Civil War veterans' pensions in the United States had.[19] The term was added to the stock of symbols linking government cash aid, demoralization, and corruption. This language was not at all foreign to Franklin Delano Roosevelt, who defeated Hoover in 1932 with a mandate for decisive federal action. The grants to states by his Federal Emergency Relief Administration (FERA, modeled on TERA) were predicated on being temporary, emergency relief measures, with applicants to be investigated by trained social workers and working in return for aid wherever possible. Roosevelt intended to wholly replace federal relief with public works projects as soon as possible.[20]

> The lessons of history, confirmed by the evidence immediately before me, show conclusively that continued dependence upon relief induces a spiritual and moral disintegration fundamentally destructive to the national fibre. To dole out relief in this way is to administer a narcotic, a subtle destroyer of the human spirit. It is inimical to the dictates of sound policy. It is in violation of the traditions of America. Work must be found for able-bodied but destitute workers. The federal government must and shall quit this business of relief. I am not willing that the vitality of our people be further sapped. . . . We must preserve not only the bodies of the unemployed from destitution but also their self-respect, their self-reliance and courage and determination.[21]

At the end of 1935, FERA was abruptly terminated. Despite suspicions that they had yielded to pressure from business interests, the evidence is that Roosevelt and his advisors acted out of fear that the continuation of federal relief was corrupting the American citizenry and could create a permanent dependent class.[22] Federal aid was thenceforth to be linked more tightly to work, aimed at willing workers and select categories of those not expected to work; responsibility for everyone else was relegated to the state and local governments. For the immediate crisis, temporary public works projects would employ as many workers as funding would allow. For the long-term, the Social Security Act instituted Unemployment and Old Age Insurance to address predictable hazards in workers' lives (and co-opt movements for national old-age pensions in the form of cash grants based on neediness). These "insurance" programs were financed by compulsory contributions from workers rather than general tax revenues, and benefits were tied to past earnings rather than need, thus attempting to guard against pressures for an ever-expanding "dole." Assistance to states' old-age pensions (Old Age Assistance) and aid to dependent children programs (Aid to Dependent Children, or ADC) was included in the Act, but this was expected to be temporary, lasting until most aged workers and widows of workers could be brought within coverage of the Old Age Insurance program. The ADC provision was an afterthought attached through the lobbying of the Federal Children's Bureau, and attracted relatively little attention at the time.[23]

By the closing years of the 1930s, some of those who had been top administrators in FERA were proposing the responsibility of modern government for its citizens' "right to work." Harry Hopkins, former head of FERA, compared the challenge of developing unsettled land in the past with the current challenge of making full use of the nation's productive resources of labor and capital.[24] As the depression seemed to finally end only by the massive government spending on World War II, economic theories which called for deliberate government fiscal policy (decisions on overall levels of spending and taxing) as an antidote to economic downturns began to gain political credibility. Fears of a return to depressed conditions at the end of the war inspired a Full Employment bill which would explicitly make it national policy to guarantee a right to a job for all who were willing and able to work.[25] Parallels with justifications for the homestead acts and for the right to property specified in the early state constitutions (when access to property was considered essential to the pursuit of happiness) were recognized by the bill's promoters:

> The bill aims at creating a dynamic approach to the problem of providing expanded production and consumption, thus creating sufficient job opportunities. The approach attempted is not dissimilar to the one taken in the Homestead Act which helped expand our system of free enterprise during the last century.[26]

> I think we settled the question of the right to work 169 years ago, in the Declaration of Independence, when we decreed that among the inalienable rights of men was the right to life, liberty and the pursuit of happiness . . . that statement of 169

years ago becomes merely a will-o'-the-wisp if in the pursuit of happiness a man cannot get a job and receive a salary with which to support his family.[27]

Critics, however, attacked the implied policy of using the national government as employer of last resort, arguing that in any severe downturn the number of jobs that would need to be created would require the government to go beyond public works projects to massive intrusion in the fields of private enterprise—that, or the creation of unproductive and thus inflationary "make-work" types of jobs.[28] The prospect of expanding dependence on the government and diminishing private economic initiative obviously violated the republican tradition. Government-guaranteed employment was thus difficult to fit to the model of the nineteenth-century land acts, in which resources were transferred from public to private hands and then the government essentially stepped out of the picture.

As finally enacted, the Employment Act of 1946 committed the national government to monitor the economy and take unspecified action to insure "maximum" employment, production, and purchasing power.[29] New means were being sought for the traditional aim of advancing the nation's economic life by providing citizens with opportunities for productive work. But the means by which the government might make work available in the modern economy, in contrast to the relatively simple proposition of parceling out the public lands to settlers, is a tremendously complex problem. In the first place, there is a multitude of options for affecting the general level of employment, including new public works projects, speeding up authorized spending, loosening credit, or cutting taxes. In the second place, as was soon recognized, some unemployment is "structural" and requires targeted interventions to be effective—such as aid to specific areas that are economically depressed, job training or retraining for particular workers, and measures to attack discrimination in employment. Finally, all of these options provoke worries about budget deficits, inflation, and the timing of interventions. Of such complicated considerations have subsequent employment policy debates been composed.[30]

3. Opportunity vs. Welfare

The chief issue in national domestic policy debates during the postwar years was avoiding cyclical downturns in employment (or, for conservatives, avoiding inflation), and little attention was paid to poverty as a separate issue. But some social workers, social scientists, and government officials were paying attention, and had come to a belief in government's responsibility in an industrial society for providing adequate incomes to all those in need. This modern version of liberalism is distinguished from its classical Lockean predecessor by its emphasis on the use of government power to expand the personal freedoms of citizens by providing them with needed resources.

There had been individuals who had held such ideas since before the turn of the century, particularly people who had studied poverty or had extensive experience with the poor, but in public debates the language of dependency and corruption had smothered the expression of alternative views. Now ongoing federal income support programs afforded strategic opportunities to shape policy incrementally, outside the spotlight of political attention. Liberal reformers, working through the Social Security Board, successfully lobbied Congress to expand Old Age Insurance coverage and raise retirement benefits for low-income workers. (Both the Board and congressional leaders saw the insurance program as a safer vehicle for expansion than the Old Age Assistance program.) Successful efforts were also made to raise the federal contribution and cover the mother in Aid to Dependent Children.[31] ADC, however, soon became an object of public controversy.

While the number of recipients of Old Age Assistance at first increased as states expanded programs to take advantage of federal matching grants, it soon leveled off and even dropped a bit as more old people became covered by the Old Age Insurance program. The numbers for ADC, in contrast, began a pattern of doubling every decade until the mid-1970s. Much of this growth was due to population increase and a general social trend towards more single-parent families.[32] In addition, massive numbers of displaced agricultural workers from the South overwhelmed job markets in the cities, which eventually began to suffer job losses because of suburbanization. ADC was the only form of aid many of these urban immigrants qualified for, once they could meet the deliberately lengthened residency requirements.[33] The end results of these factors were rising costs, a change in parental recipients from primarily widows (increasingly covered by the Old Age Insurance benefits for survivors of deceased workers) to more deserted, divorced, and never-married mothers, and a higher percentage of minority recipients.

It was a problem ripe for political exploitation, and so duly seized upon. Racial stereotypes and stereotypes about the poor reinforced one another. "Welfare," once a word meant to imply progressive administration, became attached to ADC and joined "relief" and "the dole" as a symbol crystallizing the old negative attitudes about government aid, dependency, demoralization, and corruption. It was repetitively asserted that welfare sapped the will to work, tempted fraudulent claims, and accelerated the breeding of an illegitimate dependent class.[34] The states resisted pressure from the Social Security Board's Bureau of Public Assistance to comply with liberal federal guidelines, and worked particularly hard at keeping "undeserving" mothers off their rolls.[35] Congress also became more recalcitrant, refusing reformers' efforts to mandate a national minimum benefit for ADC, contribute to the states' general assistance programs, or, until President Kennedy took office in 1961, extend ADC benefits to two-parent families.[36]

Kennedy favored the extended ADC benefits as a way to help families with jobless fathers who had exhausted their unemployment benefits during recessions. He believed that it was unfair to give ADC benefits to families of deserting fathers while refusing aid to families of fathers who did not desert. Promising to review the entire federal public assistance program, Kennedy got Congress to make ADC for families with an unemployed father a temporary option for the states. The President's study commission, made up largely of social workers, recommended higher levels of federal funding for social services to "prevent and rehabilitate" dependency, and the continuation of aid for two-parent families. In response to pressure from state and local governments, they also endorsed requiring unemployed fathers to participate in community work or job training in return for this aid.[37]

Kennedy's public statements regarding these and other recommended changes, which were successfully enacted in 1962, utilized familiar symbols but gave them a new liberal tempering. Although he sounded the traditional warning about dependency,

> This measure embodies a new approach—stressing services in addition to support, rehabilitation instead of relief, and training for useful work instead of prolonged dependency. . . . Our objective is to prevent or reduce dependency and to encourage self-care and self-support—to maintain family life where it is adequate and to restore it where it is deficient.[38]

> Unless such problems are dealt with effectively, they fester, and grow, sapping the strength of society as a whole and extending their consequences in troubled families from one generation to the next.[39]

he consistently attributed dependency to such factors as disabilities, discrimination, and lack of training, never to demoralization through the receipt of money from the federal government. (His congressional allies used stronger language, complaining that "the habit of waiting for the monthly welfare check" perpetuated the "chain of chronic dependency.")[40] Casework and work relief were traditional methods for fighting dependency, but now their focus was directed at strengthening jobs skills as much as moral character. Job training was explicitly based on the new rationale. However, even hemmed in by job training and work requirements, extending the newly renamed Aid to Families with Dependent Children benefits to unemployed men (in the act, Unemployed Parents—or AFDC-UP) was an affront to the old beliefs about cash relief and demoralization. This provision remained optional to the states, and most of them refused to implement it.

Later that year, Kennedy, who in his election campaign had characterized the Social Security Act as beginning a "war on poverty," began to see a comprehensive attack on poverty as a way of reconceptualizing and going beyond the variety of Democratic initiatives in areas such as urban renewal, job training, education, civil rights, aid to depressed regions, and combating juvenile delinquency. Various writers and social scientists were drawing attention to the persistence of poverty amidst unprecedented affluence, and Kennedy saw this as a good issue for his legislative program in the 1964 election year. Succeeding to the presidency after Kennedy's assassination, Lyndon Johnson enthusiastically embraced the idea.[41]

The specific content of the program was uncertain until the Budget Bureau hit upon local "community action programs" (CAPs), which were being experimented with in the programs fighting juvenile delinquency. The idea of federally funded but locally controlled organizations coordinating a variety of anti-poverty approaches fit the two important criteria of offering something new and keeping costs down. They could be targeted to high-poverty areas, avoiding a broader and thus more expensive program. They could pull together many initiatives under the umbrella of one "new" concept which could be more simply presented. And many of these initiatives could be programs already planned and provided for in various parts of the budget. The main thrust of the provisions of the bill followed the same services approach to tackling dependency as in Kennedy's 1962 public assistance amendments. Counseling, education, job training, and work experience, this time aimed primarily at young people, were expected to enhance abilities to take advantage of job opportunities presumed to be available. A more ambitious job creation program and proposals for expanding income maintenance were specifically rejected as too costly.[42]

Johnson had come to Congress during the Great Depression, and he adopted Franklin Roosevelt as a Presidential exemplar.[43] He characterized his War on Poverty as a second stage of the New Deal; as Roosevelt had reduced to one fifth the one-third of the nation that was "ill-fed, ill-clad, and ill-housed," he would reduce the proportion even further. He also shared Roosevelt's distaste for cash relief, and enlisted the traditional negative symbols on his side:

> It is not a program of giveaway. It is not a program of doles. It is a program that is concerned with skills and opportunities, with giving the tools for the job of growth, in making taxpayers out of taxeaters.[44]

> This is not in any sense a cynical proposal to exploit the poor with a promise of a handout or a dole. We know—we learned long ago—that answer is no answer. The measure before me this morning for signature offers the answer that its title implies—the answer of opportunity. For the purpose of the Economic Opportunity Act of 1964 is to offer opportunity, not an opiate. . . . We are not content to accept the endless growth of relief rolls or welfare rolls. We want to offer the forgotten fifth of our people opportunity and not doles. . . . The days of the dole in our country are numbered.[45]

Johnson made the Economic Opportunity Act the center of his election-year program, and the public was initially quite favorable to the War on Poverty concept. Congressional Democrats followed the President's rhetorical playbook, decrying the scandal of poverty amidst affluence and emphasizing that the bill offered opportunity, not welfare: "not a handout but a hand up." Their argument was aptly summarized by Representative Hawkins: "The purpose of this bill is to help those persons who possess individual initiative but who are without resources to make it meaning-ful."[46] These "resources" were the personal attributes economists refer to as human capital, but the parallel with providing land to the nineteenth-century poor is not hard to see. At least one congressman made the con-nection explicit:

> Escape from poverty has always required resources of one kind
> or another. During the era of America's first frontier, the
> resource was free land. I am not aware that there was any out-
> cry at the time that giving away land by the millions and mil-
> lions of acres would destroy the incentive to get ahead, or
> weaken initiative, or undermine belief in the democratic way
> of life. Today the resource has shifted from an abundance of
> free land to an abundance of productive capacity. And again,
> just as with land, the Federal Government bears the responsi-
> bility of providing access to the abundance . . . escape from
> poverty today means following the road of education and
> training and jobs.[47]

The effectiveness of the proponents' language is evidenced in the Republican opposition's repeated claim that the bill was just an election-year gimmick for attracting votes. They were forced to continually plead that they too opposed poverty, but were hard pressed to offer an alterna-tive poverty program. Instead they complained that the bill was sloppily put together, that it put more power in the hands of the federal govern-ment, that only the private sector could create the jobs that people need, and that a variety of federal programs were already addressing poverty anyway.

Johnson put his political muscle fully behind the bill to make sure it passed. The Democratic electoral landslide made renewal of the act the following year easier, but the congressional base of support remained highly partisan and was really solid only in the liberal wing of the Democ-rats.[48] Eventually conservative criticism waxed while the support of mod-erates waned. Many factors contributed to the rapid debilitation of the "War on Poverty" as a symbol that could elicit broad political support. The jumble of old and new programs under a confusing administrative structure insured problems in implementation for critics to publicize. State and local officials lost much of their enthusiasm when a little-noticed provision for the "maximum feasible participation" of the poor in

planning and running CAPs encouraged confrontational tactics by mili-
tant activists. And funding was never anywhere near adequate to fulfilling
some of the more extravagant rhetoric about abolishing poverty, as spending for the Vietnam War compounded the President's initial concerns
about the program's budgetary impact.[49]

Even so, the most important changes in the political environment
were that the War on Poverty became associated with political concessions
to African-Americans, and the negative "welfare" symbol returned with a
vengeance to dominate the discussion of poverty. The War on Poverty followed on the heels of the civil rights movement, and as African-Americans made up a disproportionate share of the poor, their leaders lobbied
vigorously to direct federal resources to their communities. When a white
"backlash" against civil rights programs developed, it carried over to the
poverty programs.[50] On top of this, the AFDC rolls did not shrink as the
anti-poverty warriors had predicted, but perversely continued their
upward spiral. In addition to the causes already mentioned, part of this
growth could be attributed to relatively wealthy northern states raising the
income threshold for eligibility, and another part to the Office of Economic Opportunity's funding of legal services, as activist lawyers succeeding in liberalizing eligibility rules through the courts and helped to
organize a National Welfare Rights Organization. But the biggest new
factor was that more eligible families applied for and successfully received
public assistance. Influenced by the civil rights movement, some poor
people began to view access to government programs as a right rather
than a demeaning favor.[51] This combination of growing expenditures for
poverty programs and an assertive constituency fit right in with the old
fear that cash assistance would corrupt politics by increasing dependence
on government aid. This fear now, however, had an unmistakable racial
subtext.

4. THE DEFEAT OF A GUARANTEED INCOME

The Kennedy-Johnson approach of offering a variety of social services
to help the poor had been presented as an attack on dependency. The traditional importance of this concept may have made such language politically effective, but it also kept the larger complex of ideas associating
dependency, government cash aid, demoralization, and corruption near
to hand. By 1967 it was standard practice for conservative politicians to

attack the Democratic administrations by pointing to the "welfare mess." The inaugural remarks of newly elected California Governor Ronald Reagan are typical:

> We are not going to perpetuate poverty by substituting a permanent dole for a paycheck. There is no humanity or charity in destroying self-reliance, dignity, and self-respect . . . the very substance of moral fiber.[52]

The shift in mood was reinforced by the fact that increasing numbers of women throughout the United States were working outside the home, eroding the ideology of women's separate sphere which had originally shielded AFDC mothers from the expectation of holding a job. In essence, the new position was that the services approach to moving people into jobs was fine, but some mothers (like the fathers in AFDC-UP) needed a push. Even though controlled by Democrats, the House Ways and Means Committee adopted this view when it took Johnson's 1967 proposal to increase Social Security benefits and added controversial new amendments to AFDC. A "work requirement" threatened AFDC mothers considered "appropriate" for work with losing their benefits (and having their children's benefits handled by a third party) if they refused to accept jobs or work training when these were available and child care was provided. Another provision sought to pressure the states to move more recipients into jobs by imposing a freeze on the proportion of children from families with an absent living parent for which the federal government would pay benefits.[53] "Is it," asked chairman Wilbur Mills, "in the public interest for welfare to become a way of life? . . . our committee felt the time had come when the taxpayers want us to be rough . . ."[54]

The bill passed the House under a closed rule prohibiting floor amendments, but liberals were able to soften the AFDC provisions in the Senate. However, the conference committee accepted the House provisions and Democrat Russell Long, the bill's floor manager in the Senate, outmaneuvered the liberals' threatened filibuster of the conference report.[55] The Congressional debates were permeated with the updated republican ethic of promoting independence, self-respect, and personal responsibility by preparing welfare recipients for employment, here illustrated by the words of Senator Long:

> Our concern is not only fiscal but human. We are worried about the effects on the human spirit of protracted periods on

> 'welfare'—periods which are beginning to stretch from gener-
> ation to generation. Because of its concern, the Committee on
> Finance recommends . . . restoring more families to employ-
> ment and self-reliance. . . . It is expected that the individuals
> participating in the program established under this part will
> acquire a sense of dignity, self-worth and confidence which
> will flow from being recognized as a wage-earning member of
> society . . .[56]

The argument was over whether such preparation for employment should
be voluntary or mandatory. Conservatives from both parties claimed the
voluntary approach was not working; liberals claimed the mandatory
approach was inhumane and would work even worse.

The new law offered something for each side. It established the Work
Incentive Program (WIN), a carrot-and-stick approach to getting adults
off the AFDC rolls. The stick was the new work requirement. The carrot
was that the benefits of recipients who got jobs would not be completely
reduced by the amount of their earnings, but only partially reduced.
"Soft" services such as counseling were de-emphasized in favor of "hard"
services (more specific and measurable) such as vocational rehabilitation
and day care so parents could train or search for jobs. The freeze on reim-
bursement for families with absent living parents was retained, although
the states (which would lose federal funds while retaining responsibility
for poor families) were able to delay and finally kill this provision. The
law also required the Internal Revenue Service to make available any
information it had on the deserting fathers of AFDC children to help
track them down for child support.[57] This built upon law in place since
the 1950s that required welfare workers to report deserted families to law
enforcement officers, and was a harbinger of further moves in the same
direction.[58]

The carrot portion of WIN came from Department of Health, Education and Welfare (HEW) staffers working with the Ways and Means
Committee, and was borrowed from the concept of a negative income tax
(NIT) developed by conservative economist Milton Friedman. In a NIT,
just as families with incomes progressively higher than a set amount are
taxed at progressively higher rates, families whose incomes dip further and
further below the "break-even" point receive larger and larger cash supplements from the government. However, if a poor family's income from
work goes up, the rate at which it loses government support is a "tax rate"

of less than 100 percent (Friedman recommended about 50 percent), which means the family is always financially better off when its members work. The main concern of federal bureaucrats at HEW and at the Office of Economic Opportunity was the liberal aim of lifting the incomes of the poor, and the NIT was just one of several possible approaches to a guaranteed minimum income which they had been studying and promoting, others being the incremental expansion of existing programs and European-style family allowances. NIT proposals had been continually squelched by President Johnson and his top political appointee at HEW, who were not at all sympathetic. Despite this hostility, the NIT work incentive idea was successfully slipped to Congress for the changes in AFDC.[59]

The 1967 amendments did not end the furor over the "welfare crisis." AFDC continued to attract negative publicity throughout the election year of 1968, during which proposals for a NIT or some other variant of a guaranteed income occasionally cropped up. The public, however, seemed hostile to such ideas, believing that "nobody should get something for nothing."[60] Robert Kennedy won cheers by attacking his Presidential primary rival Eugene McCarthy for advocating a guaranteed income, favoring instead "work, jobs, self-sufficiency and family integrity; not a massive new extension of welfare. . . ."[61] Republican candidate Richard Nixon also disavowed support for guaranteed income schemes, seeing in them a danger to self-respect and the incentive to work. One of his favorite applause lines during both his campaign and his Presidency was that "what we need are not more millions on welfare rolls, but more millions on payrolls."[62]

As President-elect, Nixon's genuine interest in the problem of welfare was reinforced by pleas from Republican governors and mayors for budgetary relief. He set up a task force of policy experts which recommended incremental reforms long favored in professional policy circles but which could be argued to address conservative concerns. Despite his putative opposition to any type of guaranteed income, the chief recommendation was one Nixon showed sympathy towards: establishing national minimum benefits fully paid by the national government for AFDC and the categoric assistance programs for the aged, blind, and disabled. This would raise benefit levels in the South, and thus (it was assumed) reduce the migration of poor blacks to the high-benefit northern states. It would also replace some of the northern states' welfare expenditures with federal funds. Another recommendation was to require all the states to implement AFDC-UP, so that unemployed fathers would no longer have an incentive to desert their families in order to get them on welfare.[63]

The negative associations of cash-aid programs were of course familiar and pertinent to the new President:

> . . . as we look through the ages, and welfare is not new, we have found that inevitably when such programs continue and escalate in any society, welfare tends to destroy those who receive it and to corrupt those who dispense it.[64]

But for policy specialists in the federal bureaucracy, the way welfare "destroyed" recipients was understood in terms of economic incentives, not moral character. Failing to offer benefits to families with fathers was an incentive for family breakups. Offering benefits to the unemployed but not to full-time employed parents with low incomes was an incentive to quit work. Taking away benefits at too high a rate as work income rose was an incentive to reduce work effort. The policy specialists did not accept the traditional view of cash aid in itself being a source of demoralization, and believed the proper mix of program incentives could solve the problems.

Nixon's HEW head Robert Finch and urban affairs advisor Daniel Moynihan (a Democrat who had long championed family allowances) favored the task-force proposals, but the President's domestic policy advisor, Arthur Burns, led an intra-administration attack on the proposals as an extension of welfare. Nixon, needing some kind of welfare reform proposal, sent the national minimum benefits idea over to HEW to be shaped into legislation. There holdovers from the Johnson administration seized the chance to work up a proposal for a NIT for all families with children at the same budgetary cost as the task-force proposal. Presented as a complete replacement of welfare which addressed the economic incentives for reduced work and family breakups, what was to become known as the Family Assistance Plan (FAP) quickly won support from Finch and Moynihan. Burns, recognizing the new alternative as a guaranteed income proposal, switched to advocating the national minimum benefits combined with more money for work training, job placement and day care, with a requirement to accept work or training where available along the lines of the 1967 law. Nixon was torn between competing views of whether FAP would be perceived as a replacement or an extension of the welfare system.[65]

Finally, repelled at the thought of mere "tinkering with the present welfare system,"[66] Nixon compromised by combining FAP with enhanced work incentives, the work requirement, and the additional job training, job placement, and day care. The widespread dissatisfaction with the current welfare system, his own desire to have an impact on the issue, and the availability of a radical alternative were the controlling features in Nixon's acceptance of what was essentially a NIT.[67] The added work features were necessary camouflage to present it with the appropriate symbolism. "I don't care a damn about the work requirement," the President confided privately. "This is the price of getting the $1,600" (the minimum guaranteed annual income for a family of four).[68]

The President presented his proposal in a nationwide television address on August 8, 1969. After carefully cataloguing its problems, he proposed to "abolish the present welfare system" and adopt a new system based on the principles of "equality of treatment across the Nation, a work requirement, and a work incentive." He described how FAP would work, and insisted that it was not a guaranteed income: "A guaranteed income would undermine the incentive to work; the family assistance plan that I propose increases the incentive to work." He defended the cost of the program as an investment in "turning around our dangerous decline into welfarism in America," and returned to his primary theme:

> And the man who now only looks ahead only to a lifetime of dependency will see hope—hope for a life of work and pride and dignity.
>
> In the final analysis, we cannot talk our way out of poverty; we cannot legislate our way out of poverty; but this Nation can work its way out of poverty. What America needs now is not more welfare, but more "workfare."
>
> The task of this Government, the great task of our people, is to provide the training for work, the incentive for work, the opportunity for work, and the reward for work. Together these measures are a first long step in this direction.
>
> For those in the welfare system today who are struggling to fight their way out of poverty, these measures offer a way to independence through the dignity of work.
>
> For those able to work, these measures provide new opportunities to learn work, and to find work . . .

Poverty is not only a state of income. It is also a state of
mind, a state of health. Poverty must be conquered without
sacrificing the will to work, for if we take the route of the permanent handout, the American character will itself be impoverished.[69]

As authors Vincent J. and Vee Burke pointed out, Nixon used variations of the word "work" sixty times in his thirty-five minute speech.[70] He
deliberately downplayed the fact that FAP would represent a massive
extension of cash benefits to the poor—higher benefits for a million and
a half current AFDC recipients, primarily in the South, and new benefits
for some thirteen million working poor (parents who worked, whose
incomes remained below the poverty line, and yet were ineligible for
AFDC). Instead, he focused on the importance of work in turning the
corner "from a dismal cycle of dependency toward a new birth of independence." The reaction of the general public (which is rarely attentive to
policy details) was overwhelmingly positive, particularly of those features
promising to reward work. Among the politically active elites, on the
other hand, the conventional ideological and interest group positions
were thrown into confusion by Nixon's tactics.[71]

Administration officials testifying before the House Ways and Means
Committee adhered to the President's emphasis on the work requirement,
work incentives, and training provisions. Chairman Mills and a bipartisan majority of the committee eventually made the same decision that
Nixon had—that the current welfare system ought to be replaced, and
FAP was the only real alternative on the table.[72] The committee report
presented familiar themes:

The bill is intended to convert the existing program from one
which results in people remaining in dependency to one
which will encourage people to become independent and self-
supporting through incentives to take training and enter
employment.[73]

The bill reached the floor of the House in April of 1970, with its supporters repeating the emphasis on the work provisions and the failures of
the current system. It passed with the help of a closed rule, but opposition was beginning to crystallize. Many liberals, not trusting Nixon, complained that the minimum income in the bill was too low, and continued

their fight against work requirements. More threatening, however, because of their greater potential strength, were the conservatives who began attacking the bill as a guaranteed income:[74]

> A Federal Government guaranteed annual income will destroy self-reliance, individual responsibility, self-respect, and the incentive to work.[75]

> To our way of thinking it may be demoralizing to remain forever on the Federal dole, but there is no doubt that such status can become habit forming to some. The vision of millions working themselves off the welfare rolls and onto payrolls is exactly that—a vision.[76]

The Senate Finance Committee was dominated by conservatives, principally from western states largely untouched by the welfare "mess" and southern states in which social relations would be impacted if FAP raised the incomes of millions of their black citizens. In the hearings on the bill, they harped on problems with the work incentives and possible evasions of the work requirement, and painted FAP as a massive expansion of welfare. Meanwhile the liberals, egged on by the National Welfare Rights Organization (current welfare recipients would not gain much of the new spending), attacked the work requirements as too harsh and the income support as too little. The bill stalled in committee, and despite administration revisions was finally killed by committee liberals and conservatives joining in opposition. A last-ditch attempt to add it as a floor amendment to another bill in the closing weeks of the congressional session also failed.[77]

When the 92nd Congress convened in 1971 the story was replayed. HEW and the Ways and Means Committee produced a revised FAP bill, it passed the House (by a smaller margin), supporters and opponents rehashed the same arguments, and the bill stalled in the Senate Finance Committee. In the meantime, the states took initiatives to trim AFDC benefits and rolls and Congress passed a set of AFDC amendments (sometimes known as WIN II) which expanded its job training programs and limited state discretion as to which recipients were appropriate for obligatory participation in work or training.[78] Nixon lauded the amendments as based on his workfare proposals, and, after quoting Franklin D. Roosevelt on how relief induces moral disintegration, asked the Congress to complete the job of welfare reform.[79] However, FAP died in the Senate the following year. Congress did pass a little-noticed provision to change the cash assistance programs for the elderly, blind, and disabled into a national guaranteed income program, but helping poor children by expanding cash payments to their able-bodied parents proved to be too controversial.[80] For programs involving those who are expected to work, plausible application of the "guaranteed income" label was political poison.

5. The Persistent Focus on Dependency

The politics of welfare over the next twenty years echoed the fight over Nixon's FAP. Presidents periodically called for radical change of the welfare system, but the end result was further incremental movements in the direction of more education, training, and job placement services with ever-tightening participation requirements. The liberal hope of a guaranteed minimum income grew fainter and fainter, as budgetary constraints and the persistent focus on dependency threw political boulders in the way of expanding cash aid to the poor.

Jimmy Carter in 1977 was the next president to tackle welfare reform, concluding that "the present welfare program should be scrapped entirely," and making his top priorities cost control, access to jobs, and work incentives.[81] Within the bureaucracy the chief policy options were a revamped NIT approach favored by HEW and a return to the guaranteed employment concept favored by the Department of Labor. A monumental bureaucratic struggle ensued, with HEWs approach derided as a politically disastrous guaranteed income and the jobs approach criticized for essentially the same reasons as the 1945 full employment bill. The uneasy compromise which emerged proposed to separate "employables" and "unemployables," with a large but limited jobs program for the former and a consolidated cash assistance program for the latter. (Most of the "unemployables" would be single mothers with young children. Cash assistance would also be available to residual employables if there were still not enough jobs.) Predictably, Russell Long and Al Ullman, the conservative Democratic chairmen of the Senate Finance and House Ways and Means committees, resisted the cash assistance part on the grounds that it was a guaranteed income. Liberals, on their side, complained that the jobs program was coercive and the wages too low. When it became clear that the cost of the program would be much higher than the administration estimate, the bill got stuck in committee.[82]

Attempts to revive a revised and scaled-back proposal the following year were derailed by the "Proposition 13" anti-tax movement whirling out of California, which made budget cutting more politically salient than reforms threatening to raise costs (as either a large jobs programs or NIT-type coverage of all poor families necessarily must). Media stories on the results of an expansion of public service employment under the Comprehensive Employment and Training Act (CETA) served once again to discredit government-funded jobs as a form of disguised welfare open to corruption. Daniel Moynihan, now a senator chairing the new Public Assistance Subcommittee of the Finance Committee, tried to push through at least some financial relief for the welfare costs of the bankrupt New York City, but this too failed to move. Moynihan (among others) had recently had a conversion experience because of the results of NIT experiments, showing reduced work effort and increased family breakups among recipients. The hearings he held on these experiments in late 1978 were a further nail in the coffin of the NIT; they seemed to confirm the traditional argument that cash aid, even with built-in financial work incentives, demoralized those who received it.[83]

The issue cropped up the following year in the final attempt to pass welfare reform legislation during the Carter years:

> . . . what we have shown in experiments that we have paid literally millions of dollars to conduct in this country, primarily the Seattle-Denver experiment, is that we get people who work less, and we have even the breakdown of families when we have a guaranteed national income in effect.[84]

The bill in question was a fallback to the liberals' incremental approach of making AFDC-UP mandatory for all states and establishing national minimum benefits. It managed to get out of committee in the House and barely survived a Republican recommittal motion which would have replaced it with block grants to the states and stricter work requirements (a preview of things to come). When the administration requested delaying the funding of a companion jobs bill because of budgetary concerns, what little enthusiasm there was for the two bills evaporated.[85]

Carter's 1980 presidential opponent, Ronald Reagan, took up the welfare reform gauntlet with campaign promises to duplicate nationally his reforms instituted while governor of California. Allowed by the national government through a special waiver, these relied primarily on tightening eligibility and mandating community service work in return for benefits (this concept appropriated the "workfare" label) in order to cut rolls and reduce costs.[86] The welfare reform plank of the Republican Party platform drew heavily on the traditional civic republican themes in attacking the Democrats:

> Our nation's welfare problems will not be solved merely by providing increased benefits. . . . By fostering dependency and discouraging self-reliance, the Democratic Party has created a welfare constituency dependent on its continual subsidies. . . . We categorically reject the notion of a guaranteed annual income, no matter how it is disguised, which would destroy the fiber of our economy and doom the poor to perpetual dependence.[87]

Reagan's victory also brought Republican control to the Senate and the replacement of thirty-five liberal Democrats with conservative Republicans in the House. Under these auspicious conditions, the new President passed an Omnibus Budget Reconciliation Act that significantly changed the taxing and spending policies of the national government, and included cuts in a wide variety of social welfare programs. As for AFDC, in addition to the lowering of its income eligibility limits, its NIT-inspired 1967 work incentive features were limited to four months after a recipient began working, and work expense deductions in income tests were severely restricted. The policy of using positive financial incentives to encourage work was thus repudiated. The administration also proposed to replace the WIN job training programs with mandatory workfare, but in this Congress would only agree to permit experiments with workfare, mandatory job search, state-designed job training, or "grants diversion" (using AFDC benefits to subsidize on-the-job training) programs at each state's option.[88]

Every year for the next six years, with the welfare debate embedded in budgetary issues, the administration sought to substitute mandatory workfare for WIN and institute further cuts in AFDC. However, the severe recession of 1982 allowed the Democrats to make an issue of the increase in poverty and helped them regain twenty-six House seats in the congressional elections. Not only did House liberals successfully resist mandatory workfare, they won modest reversals of some of the AFDC changes such as income eligibility and work expense exclusions, and even began to push for AFDC-UP once again.[89]

The administration's counter-effort to keep the poverty debate centered on the behavior of the poor rather than the behavior of the economy was aided by media attention to a putative "underclass" which lumped together long-term welfare recipients, street criminals, drug addicts, and other demoralized urban denizens.[90] Some academics also focused on behavioral problems, offering new versions of old arguments: poverty was due to the character and values of the poor,[91] or overgenerous government programs contributed to demoralization and the increase in poverty.[92] In his 1986 State of the Union address, Reagan renewed both the call for welfare reform and the association of government cash aid, demoralization, and dependency:

> In the welfare culture, the breakdown of the family, the most basic support system, has reached crisis proportions—in female and child poverty, child abandonment, horrible crimes, and deteriorating schools. After hundreds of billions of dollars in poverty programs, the plight of the poor grows more painful. But the waste in dollars and cents pales before the most tragic loss: the sinful waste of human spirit and potential. We can ignore this terrible truth no longer. As Franklin Roosevelt warned 51 years ago, standing before this Chamber, he said, "Welfare is a narcotic, a subtle destroyer of the human spirit." And we must now escape the spider's web of dependency.[93]

In announcing a task force to report a strategy for welfare reform by the end of the year, Reagan galvanized numerous other interested parties to conduct studies and issue their own reports.[94] The tendency to frame the problem as one of dependency was reinforced by the recent finding that while a large majority of those who went on AFDC left it within two or three years, there was a hardcore of long-term users who made up over half of the recipients at any point in time.[95] Most of the welfare reform reports reflected a "new consensus" increasingly promoted by policy experts in academia and government which favored a kind of social contract of mutual obligations between society and the able-bodied poor. Society, through the government, would offer interim support with services to help recipients become independent, while the recipients, on their part, would be obligated to overcome dependence through responsible behavior: finishing school, getting training, working, and so forth.[96]

Actually, this approach had been established in welfare policy for at least twenty years—arguably since Kennedy's 1962 amendments, certainly since WIN in 1967. Both of these had the government offer services to aid welfare recipients towards independence and obligated recipients to make use of the programs. The real area of development was in which recipients were so obligated—from just fathers in AFDC-UP, to "appropriate" AFDC mothers in WIN, to mothers with children six years of age and older under WIN II—and stemmed from the erosion of the idea that mothers were not expected to work outside the home. The "new consensus" was really a growing acceptance of a middle ground (job training resources) in preference to the more extreme liberal and conservative positions (guaranteed jobs / income or Reagan-style workfare), a middle ground that was the closest to the agrarian republican paradigm of offering the poor resources that, with effort on their part, gave them an opportunity for economic independence.

The House Democrats produced their own welfare reform report in 1986, and bills sponsored by members of both parties were introduced in each house. These agreed in stressing education and job training services, along with child care and transportation assistance so more AFDC mothers could participate in programs or make the transition to a job. Disagreements concerned how strict participation requirements should be and the relative responsibilities of the states versus the national government for the programs offered. Liberal Democrats in the House waged their annual fight with the administration for AFDC-UP and against cutting WIN funding, and finally gave in when Republican congressional leaders promised to consider the issues in welfare reform discussions the following year.[97] Then, in the wake of the Iran-contra scandal, the Democrats regained control of the Senate for the first time since Reagan came to office.

The report of the President's task force, released in December, recommended granting wide latitude to the states to experiment with various welfare-to-work programs. However, despite renewing the call for welfare reform in the 1987 State of the Union address, the administration was slow to release details of its plan. Congressional committees began hearings anyway, focusing on a Moynihan proposal to expedite the collection of child support from non-custodial parents (building on legislation passed a few years earlier) and to require custodial parents to participate at least part time in education, job training, or work. The National Governors' Association, led by Arkansas Governor Bill Clinton, pushed for bipartisan consensus around a plan which would require mothers with children three years old and over to participate in job preparation programs and would continue child care and Medicaid health insurance during a transition period if they found a job. Eventually attention began to center on a House bill in the Ways and Means committee which combined the widely accepted themes of child support collection, job preparation services with child care and transportation assistance, transitional assistance, and targeting programs on those at risk of long-term dependency; they added to these the liberals' old favorites, mandating AFDC-UP and national minimum benefits.[98]

The administration, of course, blasted the UP and minimum benefits provisions, invoking the NIT experiments and complaining that expanding benefits increased dependency, diminished work effort, and destroyed families.[99] House Republicans opposed expanding benefits with the same arguments, but added child support collection and federally funded job preparation provisions to the President's bill. With the middle ground thus being staked out, Democratic leaders toned down some of the liberal provisions of their bill in order to keep enough conservative Democrat support to maintain a closed rule and pass it.[100] The repetitive theme of the floor debates was the promotion of independence, self-sufficiency, and responsibility through education, job training, and work. This was peppered with Republican complaints that the bill was overgenerous in benefits and understrict with work requirements, and Democratic assertions that the proposed Republican substitute was meanspirited and punitive.

Meanwhile, in the Senate, Moynihan tried to gather bipartisan support for his bill, which reflected the same general themes as the House bill, including mandatory UP. But, unlike the House bill, in order to keep the cost down it capped spending for job preparation services at a definite amount (both bills removed such services from the appropriations process in order to better secure their funding) and contained no provisions for raising benefits. Early in 1988, the governors again lobbied both sides of the aisle to move the process forward. UP remained the most controversial issue, but some Republican support was bought in the Finance Committee with a compromise that would require states to offer eligible families six months a year of UP. In the face of a presidential veto threat, other modifications were made by the bill's sponsors during the floor debate, which again centered on praises of attacking dependency through education and job training. The veto threat also helped the passage of a Republican amendment requiring at least one of the parents in UP families to engage in workfare for sixteen hours a week,[101] which was presented as a prophylactic against demoralization: "to maintain and strengthen a real work ethic among recipients."[102] The bill, as amended, passed 93 to 3.

The conference report upon which the final legislation was based was much nearer the Senate than the House version—twice during negotiations, the House actually passed resolutions instructing its conferees to accept nothing which either cost more or "disallowed work" more than the Senate version. The main features of the Family Support Act of 1988 (FSA), which had extremely broad support and followed the established direction, emphasized education and job training services targeted on those at risk of long-term dependency (with participation now required of recipients with children three years of age and older, or one year and older at the option of each state) and strengthened child support collection from non-custodial parents. Other features gave some satisfaction to liberals on one side or conservatives on the other, but these were quite watered down. For example, liberals finally got mandatory UP after twenty-five years of effort, but only for six months a year and with workfare required of recipients. Conservatives were able to require states to involve a set minimum percentage of eligible recipients in job preparation programs, but the participation rates, although they were to be raised over time, were much lower than they had wanted. Despite the voicing of frustration from both ends of the political spectrum during the House debate over the conference report, it passed 347 to 53. The Senate "debate" was almost unanimous in lauding the report, and it passed 93 to 1.[103] Over and over attacks on cash aid programs and praise of the "new" approach were reiterated in the familiar language of dependence and independence:

> Mr. President, what we intended to do . . . was to redefine the whole question of dependency. Receiving income support is no longer to be a permanent or even extended condition but, rather, a transition to employment and an immediate gain of parental support for children.[104]

> . . . its central feature [is] a new program to provide states with the resources needed to educate and train those

on welfare for a life of work and independence. . . . By work-ing, we gain dignity, a sense of purpose and self respect. We develop skills, become responsible, and are able to advance in life to better serve our fellow man.[105]

We should help the less fortunate in our society receive the education, training and services they need to work their way out of poverty, and we will expect in return that they will take responsibility for their own plight. Unfortunately, our current system of welfare meets neither goal of empowerment or responsibility. Because of its historical origins, our current welfare system is largely a system of income support. As a result, far too many Americans have become mired in patterns of long-term dependence.[106]

6. THE END OF WELFARE

In all the debates leading up to the passage of the FSA, it was extremely rare to hear any voice questioning the education and training approach to helping welfare recipients become independent. One of the few was that of Representative Hawkins:

> H.R. 1720 assumes there are jobs in the economy for wel-fare recipients to move into. That premise is questionable for several reasons. First, in November, there were still 7.1 million Americans officially unemployed. The number of people working part time because they could not find full-time work rose to 5.5 million workers. Also, there were several million people classified as "working poor," who although employed full time, did not earn enough money to escape poverty. If these people have not found full-time work, or a job that pays more than a poverty wage, how can we expect welfare recipi-ents to do so?
>
> . . . It is extremely doubtful that we are ready to meet the challenges involved in delivering quality child care in a gigan-tic mandatory program for AFDC recipients while also pro-viding remedial education, training, or work experience. Under current budget constraints, the Gramm-Rudman tar-

gets, and other conflicting budgetary demands, the Federal Government shows no indication of being ready to invest enough and I believe most states will either be unable or unwilling to pick up the slack.[107]

These were reasonable worries. Over the next few years the growing recession led to record numbers of families on AFDC, and the states would not put up enough of their own money to fully utilize the federal matching funds for the job preparation programs.[108] The most effective job preparation programs are intensive, and thus expensive. States had the difficult task of balancing concerns about effectiveness, cost, and serving more people, all in an environment of poor economic conditions. These problems alone might insure that welfare reform would soon be revisited, but in addition, many of the peripheral and more controversial provisions of the FSA were to be delayed, phased in or phased out over the next half-decade or so, guaranteeing that welfare would again be an issue in the next presidential election.

And so it was, albeit with a new concept harnessing the traditional fears of cash aid and dependency. This new concept was not, at first, intended to displace the job training approach to reform. From the beginning of his campaign "new" Democrat Bill Clinton gave his call for "ending welfare as we know it" a prominent place meant to distance him from association with liberalism and cash aid for the poor. He maintained the middle-ground emphasis on ending dependency through more funding for education and job training programs, but added the concept of a two-year time limit on receiving benefits followed by some form of mandatory work.[109] This proved to be one of the most popular of Clinton's campaign promises. When production of a welfare reform bill was held up throughout the first year of his administration, some states began proposing time limits of their own—but not necessarily with any additional funding for job training, child care, and other services meant to aid in the transition from welfare to a job. The administration was initially held up not only by a slow appointment process and attention to budget and health care proposals, but it also had trouble deciding how to pay for such increased services, which were the price for winning enough Democrats to the time limit concept. In the meantime House Republicans offered their own more severe time limited welfare plan. Their conservative wing, aiming to shift the focus to the issue of sexual responsibility, added provisions to cut off benefits to teen parents or for children conceived while the mother was already receiving benefits.[110]

Late in 1993, President Clinton's task force on welfare reform produced a draft plan which included provisions to combat teen pregnancies, increased spending for job training and transitional services, and the time limit, but specified neither how to pay for the spending nor how long subsidized jobs or public employment could last for recipients who reached the two-year limit and could not find private-sector jobs. The latter question revived all the conundrums surrounding guaranteed jobs proposals since the Employment Act of 1946. An open-ended jobs program was potentially extremely expensive and, with new taxes taboo, budgetary rules forced the planners to raid other poverty programs to pay for their reforms. Arguments over these issues delayed the Clinton plan several more months, during which conservative and centrist Democrats began moving towards the Republican proposal, which limited public employment to three years.[111]

Clinton finally unveiled his welfare reform proposal in mid-1994. He scaled down the size and cost of the program by imposing the time limits only on recipients born after 1971, and paid for the program with the Republicans' idea of stripping legal resident aliens of many government benefits. In addition to ongoing public employment for those who reached the time limit and kept searching for private-sector jobs, it had the familiar features of previous welfare reforms: an incremental expansion of job search and job training programs, tougher penalties for anyone who refused to participate in such programs, and enhanced child support collection provisions.[112] Clinton's public statement, with its reiterations of the word "work," sounded uncannily like Richard Nixon a quarter-century earlier:

> The Work and Responsibility Act of 1994 will replace welfare with work. Under this legislation, welfare will be about a paycheck, not a welfare check. . . . Support, job training, and child care will be provided to help people move from dependence to independence. Time limits will ensure that anyone who can work, must work—in the private sector if possible, in a temporarily subsidized job if necessary.[113]

But once the welfare reform ball was in motion it would prove difficult to control, particularly in an election year. Hearings on the bill got bogged down with liberal complaints that time limits were unnecessary and Republican complaints that provisions requiring participation in work programs and discouraging out-of-wedlock births were too soft, and it never reached markup. Then the stunning Republican takeover of both houses of Congress in the November elections changed the dynamics of welfare reform decisively. The President's bill was suddenly eclipsed by the welfare reform proposal in the House Republicans' campaign document, their "Contract With America." The welfare plank, which followed the basic Clinton design of a two-year limit followed by mandatory work, had been the most contentious of those in the Contract, setting moderate Republicans interested primarily in strengthening work requirements against conservatives concerned with sexual responsibility and proposing to simply end benefits after two years rather than requiring work in exchange for them. The compromise on the latter was a limit of two years of benefits and one year on a work program, with a five-year lifetime limit on the receipt of benefits. After the election, when the Republican governors from Michigan, Wisconsin, and Massachusetts offered to ease budgetary concerns by accepting less welfare money in return for more freedom from federal requirements, the Republican leadership's focus began to shift to the idea of ending the entitlement status of AFDC entirely. (An entitlement obligates the government to provide benefits to all who meet the legal requirements, regardless of the overall cost.) By the end of the year, plans were afoot to replace over one hundred social programs with block grants to the states.[114]

However, members of Congress from both parties were leery of giving up all control over welfare programs to the states, with a particularly touchy point between Republicans being the conservatives' desire to bar funds to unwed teen parents. The bill that emerged from the House subcommittee in February replaced AFDC (and several other social welfare programs) with block grants to the states, but with conditions including time limits on benefits, no benefits for unwed teen parents and most resident aliens, and requirements for set percentages of the caseload to be in "work activities" by specific dates. The Republican majority rejected Democratic amendments in a series of partisan votes, but neither the President nor the House Democratic Caucus came out in favor of retaining entitlement status for AFDC. An only slightly modified bill passed the Ways and Means Committee and the full House, both of which rejected the consensus of the last welfare reform as embodied in Democratic attempts to add more funding for job training and similar services. The Democrats had also belatedly rallied around a substitute bill preserving the entitlement.[115] In a very partisan floor debate, the Republicans attacked the "liberal welfare dole" for creating and sustaining the "cycle of dependency," while Democrats accused Republicans of cutting aid for the poor to pay for a tax cut to the rich. Clear echoes of civic republican and agrarian republican themes, relating dependency to the corruption of democratic government or referencing the disposal of the public lands, continued to crop up:

> Mr. Speaker, yesterday, the chairman of the Ways and Means Committee pointed with pride to ancestors who came here not with their hands out, but to work. I must ask the chairman, did any of his distinguished ancestors receive free government land? . . . I guess that is not welfare.[116]

> [Liberals] do not want to change the welfare system, because they like it. They like it because it is good for them politically, and the truth of the matter is that the welfare bureaucracy and welfare recipients have become a core constituency of the national Democratic party.[117]

> I submit to you that with our current handout, nonwork welfare system we have upset the natural order. We have failed to understand the simple warning signs, we have created a system of dependency. The author of our Declaration of Independence, Thomas Jefferson, said it best in three words: "Dependence begets servitude."[118]

> We want to break the cycle of dependency and you do not. You want to keep the people of this country dependent on you so you can get reelected and reelected and reelected.[119]

As the momentum moved to the Senate, the tensions between moderates and conservatives, as well as between governors over the formula for distributing the block grant funds, began to boil over. In May, the Finance Committee approved a bill including block grants, time limits, and mandatory participation rates for work programs, but made optional to the states the controversial bans on aid to teen parents, to new children born to welfare recipients, and to most resident aliens. However, floor action was continually delayed because Republican leaders could not produce a bill mustering sufficient support from all of their factions to pass. It took until September to pass a bill, by a lopsided 87 to 12 with moderate Republicans and conservative Democrats joining forces to produce a bill closer to the Finance Committee version than the House version. They also insured the inclusion of such provisions as more funding for child care for welfare mothers who go to work and mandating that the states continue to spend state money at certain levels.[120] Once again the debate revolved around the issue of dependency, including repeated references to the familiar FDR quote about relief being a narcotic.[121]

The areas of broad agreement were quite clear before the conference committee between the House and Senate met: the replacement of the AFDC entitlement with fixed amounts in block grants to the states, time limits on the reception of benefits, and mandatory participation rates in work activities. All reflected the longstanding fear that cash aid demoralizes the poor and makes them dependent, and for many they also reflected a repudiation of a government grown too large and powerful by making people dependent on its largess. AFDC was an aberration in the long deference to such civic republican themes, and its demise had been only temporarily forestalled by the attempt to use job training programs to make its recipients independent. With his call to "end welfare as we know it," President Clinton had opened the door to another way of satisfying our republican sensibilities. The end of welfare was near at hand.

By November the conference committee had resolved most of the differences between the houses, although a disagreement over making a block grant of child nutrition programs held up their final report until December. In the meantime, a titanic struggle between the White House and Congressional Republicans over the budget reconciliation bill had sharpened partisan conflict. The conference report on welfare reform passed each house pretty much on party lines a few days before Christmas, with the Democrats attacking it for cutting too many social service programs and not providing sufficient funds to help welfare recipients find jobs. The President threatened to veto the bill if the Republicans did not negotiate with Congressional Democrats, citing problems in related provisions involving Medicaid and the Earned Income Tax Credit. In January he followed through on his threat.[122]

Welfare reform remained mired in the budget conflict well into 1996, despite the efforts of the National Governors Association to move the process along. The Republicans' attempt to block grant Medicaid along with AFDC held up real progress until mid-year, when they finally decided that passing a welfare reform bill would be a better campaign issue than having the President veto it again. Things then began to move quickly, with both houses passing bills in July. Although House Democrats voted overwhelmingly against the Republican bill, they voted for a very similar bipartisan substitute bill as part of a strategy for increasing the President's leverage in conference. By now the main features of reform were a foregone conclusion—block grants with time limits on receipt of benefits and requirements for the states to have specific proportions of the caseload in work by certain dates. The differences were over more peripheral provisions such as increasing money for job training programs and vouchers for parents to purchase supplies for their children after hitting the time limit. The bill passed in the Senate was acceptable enough to Democrats to split them 23 for and 23 against.[123] (In the debate over the Democrats' proposed substitute bill the Homestead analogy again cropped up: "The Homestead Act said what we are trying to say in this welfare bill. We want to help those who are willing to help themselves. It was good policy then. It is good policy now.")[124] With the President's last minute announcement that he would sign the bill based on the conference report, moderate and liberal Democrats similarly split 98 to 98 in the House. The bill would abolish AFDC and replace it with Temporary Assistance for Needy Families, comprised of block grants with time limits on the receipt of benefits. Needy families were no longer to be entitled to cash assistance from the federal government.[125] The President rightfully tied the end of welfare to the association of cash aid with dependency:

> When I ran for president four years ago, I pledged to end welfare as we know it. I have worked hard for four years to do just that. Today, the Congress will vote on legislation that gives us a chance to live up to that promise—to transform a broken system that traps too many people in a cycle of dependency to one that emphasizes work and independence; to give people on welfare a chance to draw a paycheck, not a welfare check.[126]

He signed the Personal Responsibility and Work Opportunity Reconciliation Act of 1996 (as part of the budget reconciliation process) into law on August 22.

7. Conclusion: Back to the Future

The welfare reform debate at the end of the twentieth century was eerily reminiscent of a century earlier. Cash aid programs are still blamed for at least perpetuating dependency, and often for causing it, mandatory work is again being instituted for able-bodied recipients, and the willingness to just cut off benefits has again found expression in law.

I have argued that much of the repetitive quality of these debates is due to the political language available for discussing poverty. There is a wealth of familiar symbols invoking first and foremost the idea of dependency: "the cycle of dependency" and "welfare dependency" are two common variations of a much-used word. Although "dependency" can be used to mean simply that people stay on welfare because they have no better financial alternatives, it more frequently invokes the older sense implying they stay on welfare because they are demoralized: lacking pride, personal initiative, foresight, self-discipline, and so forth. Every time a neutral word for cash aid has been introduced, it quickly took on the negative connotations of dependency; "relief," "welfare," and "guaranteed income" are cases in point. Metaphors of drug addiction, as in the oft-repeated quotation from Franklin D. Roosevelt, convey these connotations more vividly. This quotation, the most obvious bridge between the agrarian republican language of the turn of the century and the welfare debates of the last few decades, appears in every one of the debates over AFDC, usually multiple times.[127] I would wager that it must be the most frequently repeated quote in the entire Congressional Record. Attempts to define poverty as a lack of income have thus always been on the defensive, and cash aid programs have always been vulnerable to political attacks.

If the central issue is dependency, in its moral and not just its economic sense, the only policies which fit the problem are those that either promise to discipline the dependent or offer a means for them to become independent. Mandatory work programs (and sanctions against immoral behavior, such as denying benefits for new children of unmarried recipients) have perennial appeal as disciplinary tools, but unless they lead to independence they fall short of the traditional republican aspiration. The quest is for something the government can give poor people that will allow them to make themselves "independent" and "self-sufficient." The nineteenth-century model was distributing the public lands to settlers. In the twentieth century, guaranteed employment policies have failed to fit this paradigm because the scope of continuing government involvement was feared to result at best in a "disguised dole," at worst in tyrannical ("socialistic") government. The closest parallel to the public lands have been services such as education, job training, and job placement, which the government can distribute and then (it is hoped) step out of the picture. The perceived failure of this approach led to the abolition of the federal entitlement of cash aid to poor families.

What means can we offer in the twenty-first century to help poor people become "independent?" A century and a half ago, wage workers were regarded as dependent because they were not moving towards the ideal of independence represented by ownership of a productive asset such as a farm or a business of their own. Today, the prospect that many citizens may remain unemployed or be relegated to a constricted world of either make-work government jobs or dead-end, low-paying, no-benefit private jobs is similarly troubling in its suggestion of membership in an inferior class.[128] The contemporary ideal of economic independence is comprised of a "good" job, homeownership, and accumulating productive assets, usually in a pension. We have examined the failures of proposals to help poor people become homeowners and prepare for jobs. A last topic for consideration is proposals to help poor people accumulate one of today's primary productive assets—capital.

Chapter 5

Capital Assets and the Poor

A key component of civic republicanism was the idea that the ownership of sufficient productive assets to make one economically independent was vital to the exercise of responsible citizenship. In the nineteenth century this implied that successful democratic self-government depended upon making land ownership as widespread as possible. But the primary productive property of the twentieth century (in addition to the personal qualities economists call "human capital"—skills, education, experience, and so forth) is capital assets such as those represented by stock ownership.[1] The contemporary ideal of economic independence includes the accumulation of such assets, usually in a pension. As unusual as it might seem, there have been proposals to make capital ownership more accessible to the poor. In the 1960s, Louis Kelso used the symbols of agrarian republicanism to promote making capital ownership more accessible to the capital-poor, including low-income families, but got nowhere until changing his focus to Employee Stock Ownership Plans (ESOPs). More recently, other policy entrepreneurs have proposed increasing asset ownership by poor people via encouraging microenterprises or creating Individual Development Accounts. The agrarian republican tradition is also discernable in these efforts, which have just recently begun to attract political attention.

1. THE CAPITALIST MANIFESTO

A seminal figure in efforts to broaden the ownership of capital in the United States was a lawyer and investment banker named Louis Kelso. His primary practical legacy was the invention of leveraged ESOPs, but the underlying insight has broader applications. This insight was that, as capital assets pay for themselves out of the income derived from their contribution to production, even people with insufficient income to invest can become capital owners if given access to credit—by borrowing money to invest and paying the loan back through the investment's income. The concept is derived from the way many businesses obtain new productive capital: borrowing money by using the equipment to be purchased as collateral, and paying off the loan through the additional revenues generated by this equipment. In expanding this concept to benefit ordinary citizens, capital assets planned but not yet created are regarded as analogous to unsettled land. The proper channeling of credit can favor the "landless" over "speculators" by making it possible for them to stake a claim to new capital formation. According to Kelso, broadening the ownership of capital thus need not mean expropriating or redistributing currently existing capital (or inducing people to save out of meager incomes), for by influencing the methods of financing capital formation, the government can control whether capital is becoming more concentrated or more widely diffused over time.

Kelso's ideas first found a wide audience in the 1958 best seller *The Capitalist Manifesto*, coauthored by the well-known philosopher Mortimer Adler.[2] In it they argued that the continuing advance of technology means that capital assets (primarily machines) have been contributing progressively more and more to production, while physical labor (as distinguished from technical and managerial labor) has been contributing less and less. The mismatch between increased productive capacity and the decreasing proportion of income going to ordinary laborers led to the crisis in sustaining sales that contributed to the Great Depression. The response of industrialized nations has been to increase the income distributed to laborers through policies such as government-stimulated employment (for example, subsidized credit to aid the construction industry, defense spending, farm price supports, etc.), backing for labor union demands, public employment, and more straightforward redistributive policies. While acknowledging the necessity of government action, Kelso and Adler contended that these policies are inefficient, inflationary

and ultimately unjust because they reward people beyond their contribution to production (the amount each factor-owner would receive in a
truly free market). Their alternative solution was to spread the ownership
of capital so that people previously dependent upon labor income could
develop an additional income from capital assets. The authors claimed
that their solution is not only more efficient, but more in keeping with
traditional American values:

> . . . the universal ownership by individuals of wealth-pro-
> ducing and income-bearing property, which is capital in an
> industrial economy, is needed as the economic basis for the
> universal possession of political rights and privileges which
> come with citizenship in a republic.
> . . . The land-owning farmer had the kind of economic
> independence which, according to Jefferson, was the ideal
> basis for citizenship and for a vigorous as well as virtuous use
> of political liberty.
> Such men were not beholden to government for their sub-
> sistence or their independence. Their hold on both was inte-
> gral to their ownership of income-bearing property.
> Consequently, they were in a position to participate in gov-
> ernment as independent persons. They did not seek to endow
> government with extraordinary powers in order to give them
> freedom. On the contrary, because they had their freedom in
> their own property and in their citizenship, they sought to
> limit the powers of government to such as were necessary to
> protect their property and safeguard their rights as citizens.
> . . . in place of the land-owning farmer who was the ideal
> citizen in Jefferson's day, we need only substitute the capital-
> owning *common* man as the ideal citizen in our own day . . .
> such men have the kind of independence that is needed for
> self-government . . .[3]

The authors offered a variety of suggestions as to how such a diffusion of capital ownership could be accomplished, citing the Homestead
Act of 1862 as a precedent and model for their program.[4] But their main
proposal was modeled more on homeownership policy, and was later to
be further developed and promoted by Kelso under such labels as the
Financed Capitalist Plan, the Second Income Plan, and the Industrial

Homesteading Act. (Hereafter I will refer to it as the FCP.) At the heart of it is the above-mentioned idea of using long-term credit to finance stock purchases by households with small or no capital holdings. These households would borrow money from a financial institution such as a bank, invest that money in stock which is also used as security for the loan, and repay the loan in installments through the investment's earnings. The financed investments would be facilitated by favorable tax treatment, government or private insurance of the bank loans, and rediscounting of the loan notes by the Federal Reserve.[5]

Although this proposal might at first sight seem farfetched, Kelso had already put the underlying principle into practical application on a smaller scale. In 1956, the retiring owner of a profitable California newspaper chain had offered to sell the company to his employees, but his lawyers and bankers found it would be impossible for the employees to buy it out of their income. Kelso solved the problem by setting up employee benefit trusts that purchased the employer's stock on credit; this was possible under a 1953 Internal Revenue Service ruling allowing profit-sharing or stock-bonus plans to borrow money to purchase their company's own stock. The loan and its interest were paid off though the corporation's earnings in eight and a half years instead of the scheduled fifteen, and the trusts earned millions of dollars for the employees, the vast majority of whom put up none of their own paycheck earnings or savings. Kelso went on to make similar arrangements for other companies, eventually dubbing them Employee Stock Ownership Plans.[6] (The Kelso-style ESOP is now usually referred to as a leveraged ESOP, to distinguish it from other forms of ESOPs in which the employee benefit trust gains stock by direct contribution from the employing company or other means rather than borrowing money to purchase the stock.) At first ESOPs were only a peripheral part of Kelso and Adler's package of proposals, which centered on the FCP. The FCP was a larger-scale program that would potentially benefit more citizens than just those working in companies that choose to institute an ESOP.

2. PROMOTING THE CAPITALIST REVOLUTION

Kelso began to push his ideas wherever he was offered a forum. In 1965 Congressman Gerald Ford set up meetings with top Republican politicians, bankers, and economists, including an enthusiastic Richard

Nixon. The technical feasibility of the FCP was an issue, as the Republicans wanted a professional econometric study of the effects of implementing it but Kelso didn't have the resources to accomplish this. On the other end of the political spectrum, he gained liberal contacts through self-described "Jeffersonian" Norman Kurland, a lawyer who had been involved with civil rights and poverty programs in the federal government and in Walter Reuther's Citizens' Crusade Against Poverty.[7] A model legislative act was unveiled in a new book in 1967, and by the following year Kelso and Kurland had set up a small Washington office to lobby for their bill.[8]

As mentioned in the previous chapter, 1968 was an election year in which the growth of welfare was a central issue. Kelso capitalized on this interest by presenting his theory and practical program in subcommittee hearings on income maintenance programs. He presented his plan as an alternative to an incentive-destroying "dole," attacked government employment policies, and insisted that democracy and constitutional government depended upon the widespread ownership of productive property.[9] The general social turmoil of the time offered another political opportunity. In 1969, Kurland argued before the Senate Finance Committee that alienation from our political-economic system and lack of respect for private property, especially among young people and the poor, was caused by the lack of a real opportunity to acquire a "stake" of productive property in our economic system.[10] He recommended that low-income households be enabled to acquire stock through Kelso's plan, in continuation of an American tradition:

> Thomas Jefferson envisioned a democratic American society where every family could become economically independent by owning property. The Founding Fathers generally understood that 'power naturally and inevitably follows property' and that the institution of 'private property' was a primary shelter for an individual's civil liberties. They recognized that as an institutional check on the inevitable abuses that stem from concentrated power, 'private property' had the same potential in the economic world that the 'ballot' had in the political arena. Each placed ultimate power and responsibility directly in the hands of each citizen, where he could delegate it upwards and hold his representatives accountable for its exercise.

Under the Homestead Act, Jefferson's vision was realized. Formerly propertyless people responded with great enthusiasm to their new opportunity to free themselves economically by becoming owners of land. This historically unique 'private property' approach unleashed enormously high levels of agricultural productivity, in turn releasing millions from work on farms to enter industry. Thus, this dramatic program—possibly the most important enacted by any government in history—served as the main springboard for this nation's rapid rise to leadership in the industrial revolution and to world prominence.

When the land frontier ran out, unfortunately, we failed to convert Jefferson's sound ideas to an economic strategy relevant to an industrial era. Industrial capital—an even more significant form of capital than land—remained narrowly owned. Our major corporations continued to build a 'new frontier' of industrial capitalism—unlike land, of almost limitless dimensions—that continues to expand each year at a rate now rapidly approaching $100 billion worth of new structures, machines, and other forms of productive capital.

Physically, we have the know-how, technology, resources, and trainable manpower to build enough capital instruments to produce in abundance for all. Institutionally, however, we have not yet reconciled ourselves to that industrial frontier.[11]

Kurland also appeared before the House Ways and Means Committee that same year in the hearings on President Nixon's Family Assistance Plan.[12] He argued that it would be impossible to solve the problem of poverty as long as the focus remained exclusively on welfare and employment programs, and presented Kelso's plan as a solution that would create economic expansion, take millions of families off welfare, and bring wealth and autonomy to ordinary American citizens.

To understand the mechanics of the second income plan, try to visualize the Homestead Act of 1865 with a focus on the unlimited land frontier. If you combine that vision with the private and government machinery we employed to enable a person to buy a home—which, unlike capital, does not pay for itself—you can then begin to understand how a person without savings would easily become a capitalist.[13]

These efforts had little effect; one would expect that the far-reaching nature of the FCP and the extravagant promises made about it made politicians cautious. In addition, Kelso was increasingly drawing the ire of professional economists because of his accusations that they misunderstood the importance of the productive role of capital and his dramatic and unproven estimates of the respective productive contributions of capital and labor. Although these issues had no necessary bearing on his practical mechanisms for diffusing capital ownership, they gave "Kelsoism" the reputation of crackpot economics. A promising 1972 Kelso-inspired bill in the Puerto Rican legislature, sponsored by Governor Luis Ferre, was effectively killed by the Nobel Prize-winning economist Professor Paul Samuelson with a statement aimed at debunking Kelso's theories. The statement, however, focused on Kelso's ideas about the relative "productiveness" of capital versus labor, and evidenced little awareness of the actual details of the bill.[14]

By the early 1970s not only was Kelso getting nowhere with Congress, but promotion of his ideas was costing him a lot of money and taking time away from his law practice. To solve the latter problems, he built upon his earlier experience and established his own investment banking firm specializing in setting up leveraged ESOPs. The focus of the lobbying efforts was then shifted to tax legislation to make ESOPs more attractive to employers.[15] Subsequent testimony at congressional hearings put ESOPs in the forefront, still utilizing the symbols of agrarian republicanism, for example, calling his ESOP bill an "Industrial Homestead Act."[16] The shift to ESOPs proved to be a decisive change.

Kelso supporters succeeded in setting up a dinner meeting between Kelso and Senator Russell Long two months after Kelso's 1973 appearance before a subcommittee of the Senate Finance Committee, the committee that Long chaired.[17] The very next day, in executive session of the Commerce Committee, Long attached an amendment to the Rail Reorganization Act allowing ConRail to use an ESOP as part of its financing package.[18] Long became a fervent advocate of ESOPs and was instrumental in passing several pieces of ESOP legislation over the next several years. Long's own father had been a politician in the tradition of southern populism derived from Jeffersonian principles. During the Great Depression, Huey Long's Share Our Wealth plan had gained him a national following for his proposals to redistribute wealth and income in the United States, including one to give a "Homestead" (a financial stake) of $5,000 to every American family. In his first floor speech on ESOPs, Russell Long drew on the same tradition as Kelso had:

What was it that occurred in the 30 years from 1865 to 1895 in American economic history to simultaneously bring about the cherished objectives of rapid economic growth, full employment, gentle deflation, and the flowering of industrial innovation?

The answer, Mr. President, is that the 30-year period from 1865 to 1895 was the only time in the [*sic.*] history when a government—this Government—directly intervened to influence the pattern of capital ownership in the economy. This was the most effective period of the Homestead Acts. Congress, after a full decade of turbulent, and at times almost violent, debate, had legislated the steps to bring about the realization of the American economic dream—the accumulation, over a reasonable working lifetime, of a holding of productive capital that would provide significant income and economic security, as well as the economic underpinnings for political democracy . . .

I am convinced we cannot retain our economic greatness if we do not now apply the wisdom of the Homestead Acts to economic enterprises as a whole and to institute steps that will make it possible, within a few years, for every household and individual in America to become an owner of a viable holding of productive capital.

. . . we can steer a middle course, getting back to the original road that was opened by Jefferson, Adams, Madison, and other Founding Fathers, and expanded by Lincoln under the then revolutionary homestead programs. This was the essence of the American dream that sparked the hope of the property-less everywhere and worked so well before our land frontier closed. The third road opened by our pioneer ancestors was intended to make everyone a "have," an owner of income-producing property; it was intended to provide each person a stake to help him become independent of others for his subsistence and thus providing the economic foundation for a free and just political democracy. This road ended when our geographic frontiers ran out and our industrial frontier began.[19]

ESOP legislation as a starting point for broadening capital ownership was a simpler proposition than instituting the FCP, because it was incremental in nature and built upon existing tax laws (the province of Long's committee) regarding employee benefit trusts. It was also a better fit to the agrarian republican tradition because, unlike the FCP, it clearly acknowledged the value of work. Homesteaders, after all, were not supposed to receive rent from their free land; they were expected to exercise valued virtues—work, self-discipline, planning, thrift, and so forth—to reap rewards from the property. Because Kelso's financed trusts can make virtually anybody a beneficiary, a key policy choice is determining who should fill this role. Making poor people beneficiaries would enable them to become property owners, but without necessarily requiring them to exercise the virtues associated with successful ownership. Precisely because ESOPs tie reception of stock to working for the company that issues the stock, they are more politically attractive. The workers will presumably work harder and be more productive because they are (part) owners of the capital they work with, and they seem to deserve a share in the profits of a prospering company. By the time of his appearance before the Finance Committee's subcommittee, Kelso had begun to emphasize tying the provision of credit for purchasing stock to employment status in order to maintain incentives to work,[20] even though there was no necessary connection between employment and the financed investments. (In both leveraged ESOPs and the FCP the loans are paid off by the investment income; in neither is the beneficiary responsible for repayment out of other income or assets.) This concern for the work ethic would have been music to the ears of Senator Long, who had been a leading proponent of work requirements in the recent welfare debates.

3. A Brief Moment in the Spotlight

The 1970s had brought a decline in productivity accompanied by simultaneously high unemployment and inflation, ending the two decades of relatively benign economic conditions which followed the end of World War II. Management of the economy was a central political issue by mid-decade, and a variety of policy ideas competed for acceptance. Republican President Gerald Ford favored tax cuts, cuts in government spending, and incentives for new capital formation. Congressional Democrats, led by Senator Hubert Humphrey, called for economic planning and government-guaranteed jobs. There was not widespread confidence in any of these familiar policy options. Thus, when Kelso's ESOP concept, now with signs of important political support, was offered as a solution to the economic problem (particularly its aspects of low productivity and the need for new capital formation), it shot briefly to the surface of the national political agenda.

In the beginning few politicians knew much about ESOPs, for Senator Long's initial successes in ESOP legislation had been minor attachments to bills with other purposes. However, his constant pushing of ESOPs as a cure for America's economic ills had begun to draw media attention in 1974, leading to Kelso's appearance on television's *60 Minutes* in March of the following year, which made ESOPs a national media item.[21] In the summer of 1975, President Ford included a proposal for broadening capital ownership in his package of tax law changes, but instead of Kelso's leveraged plans his Treasury Department offered tax-favored savings plans.[22] When the package reached the Senate Finance Committee Long recaptured the initiative. He conditioned the expansion of investment tax credits—essentially a government gift to the current stockholders of companies making capital expenditures—on allowing an extra 1 percent credit if it was paid into an ESOP. This became known as a TRASOP (Tax Reduction Act Stock Ownership Plan) and, unlike the leveraged ESOP, was funded primarily by this government tax subsidy. The provision was for one year only, but signaled that Long intended to keep the spotlight on ESOPs.[23]

In December Senator Humphrey, the chair of the Joint Economic Committee (JEC), scheduled two days of hearings on ESOPs and on the concentration of wealth in the United States. Virtually no dissent from the aim of broadening capital ownership emerged during the hearings, but ESOPs were heavily criticized as a vehicle towards this end. Among other problems, ESOPs limit the number of new stockowners to employees of the few companies which choose to institute them, ESOPs have generally distributed stock in proportion to pay, benefiting the most highly paid employees such as company executives more than the lower-pay wage earners, ESOPs are not diversified investment vehicles, which makes them dangerous when substituted for other employee benefit plans, and ESOPs arouse labor union suspicions that they are a tool for dividing employee loyalties. Although none of these criticisms would apply to Kelso's broader plan (the FCP), very few people realized that Kelso's ideas went any further than ESOPs. A staff study summarizing the hearings and evaluating alternative ways to broaden the ownership of capital was commissioned for the following year.[24]

That spring the JECs annual *Joint Economic Report* was released, including a three-page section entitled "Broadening the Ownership of New Capital."[25] Among its recommendations was the following:

> To provide a realistic opportunity for more U.S. citizens to become owners of capital, and to provide an expanded source of equity financing for corporations, it should be made national policy to pursue the goal of broadened capital ownership. Congress also should request from the Administration a quadrennial report on the ownership of wealth in this country which would assist in evaluating how successfully the base of wealth was being broadened over time.[26]

In June, the staff report on proposals for broadening stock ownership was released, reviewing four main alternatives: ESOPs, Wage Earners' Investment Funds (used in parts of Europe and financed by a tax on employers' payrolls or profits), the FCP, and a Capital Formation Plan (CFP) also based on Kelso's ideas but eliminating his reliance on credit to create new stockowners.[27] The staff report, supervised by a professional economist, gave a qualified endorsement to the FCP and the CFP. They were concerned with the scope of the changes proposed by the FCP rather than the substance of the plan, and thus recommended incremental implementation, ongoing evaluation, and further discussion.[28] But despite this favorable evaluation and the bipartisan support for broadened capital ownership, no politician took up promotion of the FCP (or the CFP) as a serious policy option. With the presidential candidacy and election of Jimmy Carter, attention returned to the traditional Democratic economic prescription of government activism to expand employment, and the idea of broadening stock ownership was crowded off the national policy agenda. Incremental additions to the body of ESOP legislation continued,[29] and Kelso and his associates went on testifying before various congressional committees, primarily on ESOPs but sometimes bringing up his broader stock ownership plans.[30] However, the FCP has not yet had another window of opportunity for serious political attention such as the one that seemed to open in 1976.

4. ASSETS FOR THE POOR

In the late 1980s, new policy ideas to help poor people become owners of productive assets began to come together in a still ongoing movement to redirect poverty policy from "income-based policy" to "asset-based policy," a concept inspired by the writings of Professor Michael Sherraden.[31] Dr. Sherraden's ideas about asset-based policy were provoked by interviews with AFDC recipients that he conducted during the 1980s. He contrasted their common complaint that welfare kept them "trapped" and unable to move ahead financially with his own experience of accumulating assets through the structured savings of an employer-provided retirement account. He realized that most middle-class citizens accumulate assets because there are policies structured to make this easier for them, such as tax deductions for contributions to a retirement account or for the expenses of homeownership. Poor people, on the other hand, have policies based only on providing income support, policies that are usually counterproductive to building assets. For example, statutory limits on the maximum amount of assets welfare recipients can own create a disincentive for them to save.[32]

Sherraden proposed to structure asset accumulation by poor people through special savings accounts exempt from the AFDC asset limitations. These "Individual Development Accounts" (IDAs) would be dedicated to designated purposes such as buying a first home, tuition for college or job training, or retirement, with restrictions on the withdrawal and use of funds comparable to how Individual Retirement Accounts (IRAs) work. To encourage saving and to help build the assets faster, a nonprofit and / or a government agency would deposit contributions to the IDA in proportion to the amounts saved by the account holder, up to some maximum amount. The accounts would also be supervised and withdrawals cosigned by the sponsoring agency. Sherraden theorized that as asset ownership develops it has important positive effects on personal behavior, affecting household stability, future-orientation, the willingness to take risks, the sense of personal efficacy, political participation, and other characteristics. In other words, asset ownership makes better citizens. His family still handed down memories of obtaining land through the Homestead Act, and he was familiar with the affinity of his ideas to traditional republican themes, citing the "Jeffersonian ideal of agrarian republicanism" as well as the Homestead Act in support of asset-based policy.[33]

Sherraden shared his early writings on asset-based policy with a friend at the Progressive Policy Institute, a think tank affiliated with the Democratic Leadership Council (DLC), and from there they reached the Corporation for Enterprise Development (CFED), a nonprofit organization promoting microenterprises.[34] Microenterprises are extremely small-scale business operations (less than five workers, including the owner) with very low initial capitalization costs, such as (in the United States) home-based services in hair styling, auto repair, or domestic services. Very small business operations have, of course, been around for a long time, but only fairly recently have deliberate policy measures to promote their creation been developed. Typical proposals are capitalization loans and technical support to poor people who could start such a business, ideas developed for use in underdeveloped nations and later transferred to the United States. CFED was running microenterprise demonstration projects in several states, and in grappling with welfare asset limitations and other public policy concerns they had developed contacts with the House Select Committee on Hunger.[35] Seeing the compatibility of Sherraden's ideas with their proposals (for example, IDAs could also be used to fund microenterprise start-ups), CFED published an article by Sherraden in their newsletter, which led to wider media attention. These various organizational connections and the resulting publicity brought asset-based policies to the attention of several national politicians.[36]

For one, Secretary of Housing and Urban Development Jack Kemp connected Sherraden's ideas to his quest for privatizing public housing and began speaking of a larger asset-based program for poor people, eventually setting up a briefing for President Bush.[37] Another was Democrat David McCurdy, a member of the House of Representatives' "Mainstream Forum," who announced on the floor of the House the DLCs endorsement of policies to build individual ownership of assets, specifically naming ESOPs and IDAs.[38] Eventually staffers of the Select Committee on Hunger brought IDAs to the attention of new committee chair Tony Hall, who was looking for issues to help make his mark and had already shown interest in microenterprises. In May of 1991, Representative Hall introduced an omnibus antihunger bill including provisions for microenterprises and for IDA demonstration programs, the "Freedom From Want Act."[39] In testimony before the Select Committee proponents of asset-based policies again drew from the agrarian republican tradition. They praised such policies as moving poor people from "dependency to self-sufficiency," as being for the twenty-first century "what the Homestead Act was to the nineteenth," and as giving poor people a "greater stake in their communities."[40] Professor Sherraden testified in the same spirit:

Permit me to begin with a personal reflection. Two weeks ago, I was in Kansas for my grandfather's funeral. He died at the age of 100. In his later years, as old people sometimes do, he talked a lot about his childhood. He remembered his father telling him to save and have; the phrase was, "Save and have." These were very simple words, but they carried a deep meaning, I think, of ownership, security, participation, and citizenship, ideas that helped to build this Nation.

My great-grandfather, the one who said, "Save and have," was an immigrant who fought in the Civil War, and following the war he homesteaded in Kansas. He was given 160 acres of land by the Federal Government. He worked hard, married, had children, put food on the table, he saved a little, and he left the next generation a little better off.

In my view, my family was and continues to be the beneficiary of a very sensible public policy of the nineteenth century, investing in the American people to help them build assets, own property, and have a stake in America.

I cannot help but wonder how different our nation might be today if following the Civil War, freed slaves had been given the 40 acres and a mule that was talked about at the time but was not delivered.

In the early years of our republic, Thomas Jefferson said that small property ownership was the key to the success of a participatory democracy. When people own property, Jefferson believed, they become stronger members of the community.

It is a kind of paradox that individual ownership of property is so tied to community involvement, but we see examples all around us. Property owners are more likely to take an interest in the neighborhood, more likely to vote, and more likely to assume leadership positions in the community.

In Jefferson's day, owning property meant owning agricultural land for farming. Today, we are no longer a nation of farmers, but there are important forms of asset accumulation that the Federal Government can and should support, and doing so would be sensible policy based on fundamental American values.[41]

From this point on references to microenterprises and IDAs began to pop up regularly in bills, amendments and congressional speeches. Occasionally they were incorporated into a larger asset-based policy agenda; for example, Democratic Representative Mike Espy presented a program composed of microenterprises, IDAs, ESOPs, and the privatization of public housing.[42] The chief selling point of asset-based policy was that it was geared to counter the dependency of income-based welfare. It would "change the rules so as to foster independence and not dependency," and "help low-income individuals help themselves and move from economic dependency to self-sufficiency";[43] "Instead of fostering dependency, it promotes independence and self-sufficiency."[44] Agrarian themes originally based on landholding also crop up: "Assets and investments make people stakeholders in our society, and our society is strongest when everyone has a stake in it."[45]

States began obtaining asset limitation waivers for their welfare programs from the federal government in order to allow experiments with asset-based policy, and inevitably the ideas became implicated in the movement towards welfare reform. Presidential candidate Bill Clinton, a member of the centrist DLC looking for ideas to disassociate himself from traditional liberal position on welfare, endorsed IDAs and microenterprises in his important "New Covenant" speech early in his campaign.[46] When President Clinton's task force on welfare reform began working on a bill, the stress was on time limits for the receipt of welfare, and at first it looked as though asset-based policy would be neglected. But Bruce Reed, the domestic policy advisor in charge of welfare reform, had been a supporter of IDAs when working with the DLC before the election. He allowed former Representative Mike Espy, who had become Secretary of Agriculture, to place an aide on the task force to push IDAs.[47] An IDA provision was included in the proposal,[48] but, with the election of a Republican Congress, the President's plan was shunted to the sidelines. Still, asset-based policy had already proven to have bipartisan appeal, and IDA and mircoenterprise provisions turned up in several of the other welfare reform plans in play in the Congress.[49]

Ultimately, due to an amendment offered by Republican Senator Dan Coats and passed without objection, an IDA provision was included in the Republican welfare reform bill that was signed into law in 1996.[50] The Personal Responsibility and Work Opportunity Act provides that states may use their block grant funds to carry out IDA programs, including cocontributions to accounts if a state chooses. Accounts must be used for educational expenses, buying a first home, or starting a microenter-prise. For those states that do not fund IDAs directly, they can allow the establishment of IDAs funded by the private sector—community organi-zations, churches, businesses, or other sources. Savings must be from earned income, but the savings, cocontributions and interest in an account would all be exempt from welfare asset limitation requirements.[51]

By mid-1997 twenty-four states had included provisions for IDAs in their welfare reform plans, and over two hundred community-based IDA programs had been established. That same year CFED launched a multi-million dollar nationwide IDA demonstration and evaluation program funded by a group of foundations, planning about two thousand IDAs in over ten communities. An organization headed by Professor Sherraden developed the evaluation instruments.[52] The momentum of interest in IDAs carried over into the Assets for Independence Act, a descendent of the bill originally introduced by Representative Hall in 1991 and revived periodically since then. The act provides for a five year, $125 million demonstration and evaluation program, establishing fifty thousand IDAs across the nation. In addition to excluding IDA assets from federal wel-fare programs' asset limitations, it provides for the tax deductibility of contributions to and the tax exclusion of distributions from IDAs.[53] The bill attracted strongly bipartisan coalitions and passed by wide margins in both houses (in the Senate by unanimous consent, and in the House 346 to 20). President Clinton signed the act into law on October 27, 1998.

5. CONCLUSION:
CONNECTING ASSETS AND VIRTUES

Capital is a primary productive asset in our time, yet its ownership remains highly concentrated in the hands of a wealthy minority.[54] One can imagine that if poorer citizens had a greater opportunity to develop a significant capital stake in the contemporary economy, their increased economic security and independence would also increase their political potency and perhaps the exercise of civic virtues as well. The two politi-cal movements covered in this chapter have made this argument; their reliance on the language of civic and agrarian republicanism has been detailed in this chapter.

In proposing to use credit to make poor people capital-owners, Kelso ran into a problem in the analogy between owning land and owning capital. A nineteenth-century settler may have bought public land with cheap credit, but he had to work and sacrifice in order to make that land into a productive farm. Kelso's Financed Capitalist Plan severed the tie between ownership and sacrifice, and thus suffered from the suspicion that it was an illusory "free lunch."[55] On the other hand, leveraged Employee Stock Ownership Plans, which tie ownership to work, have attracted political support and become a practical success. It is not likely, however, that ESOPs will become widespread enough, particularly in the businesses where low-wage workers are employed, to make much of a dent in the problem of poverty.

The more recent effort to develop an asset-based policy program for poor people has drawn upon the republican ethical tradition more artfully. Unlike a loan to purchase stock, a loan to establish a microenterprise requires work and sacrifice on the part of the borrower in order to produce a revenue stream to repay the loan. And while relatively few poor citizens might be potential microentrepreneurs, most could find ways to save a little in an IDA. Not only do IDAs require sacrifice, they orient their owners to the building of further assets such as owning a home or the development of human capital through education or work training. As many have recognized, IDAs could be a potential foundation for a broader program for spreading asset ownership to poor citizens. The next and final chapter further discusses such a policy program.

Chapter 6

Conclusion: Independence in a Postindustrial Economy

My thesis has been that U.S. poverty policy has been significantly affected by an ethical tradition derived from civic republicanism, and that changing economic conditions have rendered modern applications of this tradition incoherent. I traced the tradition from the U.S. founding period and the debates over the public lands to its adaptation to policies regarding homeownership, welfare, and broadening capital ownership. In the introductory chapter, I set forth as the aim of this history a "stepping back" from the tradition in order to examine its premises, its limitations, and its potential for a more rational usage. My broader goal was described as contributing to the public discussion of poverty policy rather than extracting generalizations about policy processes. In this concluding chapter, I want to discuss the results of the research and offer some policy suggestions aimed at bringing the civic republican tradition into greater coherency in its application to poverty policy in our contemporary world.

1. The Unraveling of an Ethical Tradition

A recurrent theme in the presentation of my research has been the problems of coherency that can arise when an ethical tradition which made sense in particular social circumstances is carried into conditions that are dramatically different. Packed into the meaning of land ownership in the nineteenth century were at least three important concepts which became separated in the industrial economy of the twentieth century. Land gave its owner geographic rootedness (a "stake" in a community), an opportunity for useful labor, and a productive asset offering financial independence. These concepts connected land ownership to a moral ideal of citizens who are committed to the community in which they live, who work hard and exercise foresight, thrift and other virtues to improve their economic position, and who are economically independent of the control of others, particularly government officials. Whether land ownership actually helped develop such qualities and whether land policies really made land ownership a viable option for most citizens can be questioned, but at least the argument could be taken seriously as making logical sense in the way it connected property ownership to the moral ideal.

In the twentieth century the most coherent use (and the biggest effect) of this tradition in the political discussion of poverty issues has been in defining the problem as one of dependency, with all the connotations of bad citizenship that word conveys. Dependent people, propertyless and usually unemployed, the tradition insinuates, are not committed to the community, do not exercise key virtues, and cannot be trusted to make decisions about their own lives, let alone political decisions. Correspondingly, it has been very difficult to advance a definition of the problem framed in the terms of the most important rival tradition, modern liberalism: that poverty is a lack of money most directly solved by income maintenance programs. Opponents of such programs draw upon the republican tradition to attack them as perpetuating dependency. Income maintenance programs may be acceptable if the recipients can be defined as disabled and so incapable of economic independence, or if the program can be defined as "self-help" in the form of a contributory insurance program (e.g., Social Security's Old Age Insurance), or if there is a counter-tradition that puts dependency in a positive light (as the early proponents of Aid for Dependent Children programs argued that a woman's economic dependency was for the sake of devoting herself to the sphere of homemaking and child care). But for able-bodied adults who are expected to be economically independent, a category that today includes single mothers of young children, the republican tradition has made noncontributory cash aid programs easier to attack than defend.

What then, according to the republican tradition, should be done with poor able-bodied adults? This is the flip side of the tradition: if dependency is the problem, what does it mean to be independent, and how do people achieve this status? In the nineteenth century independence meant land ownership, and thus the poor were offered free or inexpensive land. If any then failed to take advantage of the opportunity to obtain land and become independent, social condemnation and the discipline of mandatory work could be justified. But what kind of opportunity could we offer the poor in the twentieth (and twenty-first) century? Land ownership no longer carries the meanings that it once did, and the concepts associated with republican independence have unraveled into separate strands. Homeownership gives geographic rootedness, a job permits one to exercise the virtues related to useful labor, and capital assets provide the security that frees one from control by others.

As was pointed out in the earlier chapters, when these different goods are considered piecemeal as aims of policies to bring poor citizens to republican independence, the tradition becomes incoherent. Helping poor people to become homeowners may give them a greater sense of a stake in the community, but it will not provide economic independence. And while in today's world a job affords useful work and a form of economic independence, if that term is restricted to mean independence from government or charitable cash support, it has been hard to come up with government programs to help poor people obtain jobs without contradicting the premises of the tradition. Proposals for government-guaranteed jobs suggest a level of continuing government intervention in the economy that is hard to reconcile with the republican aim of keeping government under control by making people economically independent of it. Jobs that are directly funded by the government are also open to the suspicion that they are merely "make-work" and not really useful jobs, a kind of disguised welfare in which the poor remain dependent upon government aid. On the other hand, job search and job training programs do not imply continued dependency or extensive intervention into the economy, and thus have been an attractive alternative. However, this attraction fades if the programs do not actually result in removing significant numbers of welfare recipients from the rolls, as when there is a lack of job opportunities for the trainees.

But in better economic times when more jobs are available and poor people *are* moving into the work force, simply having a job still falls short of the full meaning of republican independence. A low-paying, no-benefit, insecure job is not what Americans generally mean by achieving economic independence, and is unlikely to do much to inspire the traditional civic republican virtues. Modern Americans ideally expect there to be a ladder for hard workers to climb towards finding a better job, becoming a home-owner, and accumulating capital assets for retirement (and to leave some-thing for their heirs). Poverty policy attention has been so focused on the negative side of the republican tradition—avoiding dependency on govern-ment cash aid programs—that the positive side of the tradition—providing ladders towards greater independence—has not gained commensurate attention. Economic independence means having increasing control over one's financial circumstances and is predicated on building assets over time, much as a pioneer would take a piece of uncultivated land, clear it, plow it, build on it, and gradually turn it into an income-producing farm. A very few analysts have proposed policies to aid the poor in accumulating assets, and one of the lessons learned is that such policies must be linked to virtu-ous behavior such as working and saving in order to remain faithful to the tradition. Thus, although Kelso's Employee Stock Ownership Plans were relatively well received, his Financed Capitalist Plan was not.

2. REWEAVING THE STRANDS OF THE TRADITION

To bring the civic republican tradition back to a level of rational coherency when applied to contemporary issues of poverty, the proxi-mate policy aims would incorporate all three of the strands which were once woven together but have now become separated. The overarching aim of the tradition is to support self-government by producing a par-ticular type of citizen. A coherent tradition would link government poli-cies to the desired civic virtues in a logical fashion. Whether these policies would actually affect citizens in the way desired is also impor-tant,[1] but first we must be able to make sense of the moral justification for the policies. As indicated above, there are multiple goods needed for the poor to achieve the republican ideal in today's world: useful work combined with the accumulation of assets in the form of a home and capital holdings. It could logically be argued that a citizen in such a posi-tion would exercise the virtues related to working and to caring for prop-erty, be committed to a specific community, and have some measure of the economic security that allows the development of independent polit-ical judgment. As Michael Sherraden has pointed out, we already have policies in place for the middle class (and the wealthy) to help them build assets in the form of a home and a retirement account. Unfortunately, because these benefits are largely based on tax deductions they are for the most part inaccessible to people who are underemployed or in low-wage jobs.[2] There remains a large gap on the ladder to independence just above the bottom rung.

A favorite policy approach of many contemporary analysts seeking to help those on the bottom rung has been the idea of "making work pay." This is essentially an effort to raise the incomes of the working poor, for example, by increasing the minimum wage or supplementing low wages through tax credits. From the perspective of the republican tradition these policies are inadequate because they do not lead to economic independence, and could even be attacked as enlarging government power or creating new forms of dependency.[3] The larger the benefit, the more susceptible the policy is to attack. The Earned Income Tax Credit is a case in point. A descendent of the negative income tax, this policy of giving refundable tax credits to low-wage workers with children was initially backed by members of both parties as an offset for a raise in Social Security payroll taxes. But when liberals began trying to expand the size of the credits, conservatives turned against the EITC as another government cash aid program. Furthermore, to return to the point about economic independence, these policies do little to make accessible to low-wage workers the benefits that help middle-class workers accumulate assets. The republican tradition is more than a "work ethic," and involves more than having a minimally adequate income. If people have slightly higher incomes but still little or no prospect of accumulating assets, we have failed to make republican independence possible for them.

It is in this respect that the new asset-based policies described at the end of chapter 5 are promising, particularly Sherraden's Individual Development Accounts. It will be helpful before further discussing the potential of the IDA concept to first sketch out how the typical IDA works.[4] (Bear in mind that at the time of this writing there are a variety of forms of IDAs being experimented with under various names by states, local communities, and nonprofit organizations, and standards for successful designs are just starting to emerge.)[5] A qualifying poor person sets up a savings account in a participating financial institution, with a parallel account set up and controlled by a private nonprofit or a public agency. Together these accounts comprise the IDA. The individual deposits savings on a regular basis, perhaps via payroll deduction, and also participates in financial education and counseling sessions conducted by the sponsoring agency. The agency deposits cocontributions in the parallel account at some designated ratio to the amount of the savings deposits, up to some predetermined maximum. Money in the IDA will be withdrawn in tandem by the account holder and the sponsoring agency for a designated purpose such as education or job training, down payment on a first home, or a microenterprise start-up, paid by check to the vendor(s). (Retirement income is not a designated purpose under the welfare reform act.) There are generally provisions for emergency withdrawals from the individual account, but not the parallel account holding the cocontributions. Withdrawals from the individual account under any other conditions entail forfeiting the money in the parallel account, and possibly other penalties. Funds in both accounts, including interest earned, are exempt from asset limitations of welfare programs, and perhaps from federal, state, and local income taxes.

IDAs are promising as a poverty policy that updates the civic republican tradition because they are aimed at helping the poor build assets, and in such a way as to bring the three strands of the tradition (work, homeownership, and productive property) into relation with one another. The cocontributions provide an incentive for poor people to engage in valued behaviors such as working, saving, and planning for the future, while restrictions on the use of the funds orient the account owners towards asset-building goals such as education (developing human capital), homeownership, or starting a microenterprise. Insofar as they help people along a path that includes work, homeownership, and accumulating productive assets (in a microenterprise or, possibly, as retirement investments), IDAs can be joined coherently to republican ideals.

IDAs are also promising because they could converge with various other tax-favored saving and investment accounts, creating a bridge for the poor to enter an emerging world in which individual investment accounts are becoming an important feature of social policy. IDAs have obvious affinities with policy ideas such as expanded Individual Retirement Accounts, also known as Super-IRAs (permitted to fund education and homeownership as well as retirement), 401(k) retirement accounts, educational savings accounts, President Clinton's proposal for Universal Savings Accounts (more on this below), and so forth. In our postindustrial economy, where a lifetime job in a single company is becoming extremely rare, there is a need for social policy to change from encouraging company-specific benefits towards encouraging individualized benefits programs.

Retirement benefits are moving from defined-benefit to defined-contribution plans, and should eventually become more portable, moving with workers from job to job. In the future retirement accounts may also serve when needed as a fund to pay for job skill retooling or as a cushion of savings between jobs, as well as being a possible springboard to higher education and homeownership. Such multipurpose individual investment accounts may well play in the twenty-first century a role analogous to that of land in the nineteenth, a productive asset that grows more valuable over a citizen's working life and affords her or him economic security and independence. But without something like an IDA acting as a new Homesteading Act, the poor will be left further and further behind as the rest of us enter the frontiers of this new economic world.

3. Independence for the Poor in a Postindustrial World

Let me offer a vision of what such a multipurpose individual investment account could become, drawing once again on the analogy with the role of land in the nineteenth century. I will use the term Universal Savings Account (USA) for these accounts, and later distinguish them from President Clinton's USA proposal. Until President Clinton picked up the term for his proposal of government subsidies for retirement accounts targeted on lower-income workers, the term Universal Savings Accounts was used by the Corporation for Enterprise Development to promote a vision of a multipurpose savings account somewhat similar to what I will be describing.[6]

For most Americans a century and a half ago, work meant working on the land. The aspiration was to gain a piece of land of one's own, whether by inheritance, gift from relations, purchase after working and saving, homesteading public land, or purchase through credit. Once a person owned land, their work would be aimed at continually increasing the productiveness of this primary asset. The land at first might provide only fruit, nuts, and small game, barely enough to live on. But over time the owner would clear and plow more and more acreage, replace a temporary shack with a permanent house, and acquire tools and animals to increase productivity. In times when produce markets were disrupted one might live off the land until better times returned. The owner would hope eventually to retire on the income provided by a mature farming operation, perhaps manned by hired hands. At death one would have something to leave to heirs, giving them a head start towards economic security and republican independence.

Correspondingly, work in the twenty-first century should aim at building up a USA of one's own, essentially an individually owned, tax-protected savings and investment account for asset-building purposes. A USA might initially be funded through a variety of means, similar to those for acquiring land: inheritance of parents' assets, gifts from relations or others (including nonprofit agencies aiding the poor), regular paycheck withholdings or contributions by an employer (the evolution of retirement benefits), government subsidies, or non-recourse loans (as Kelso proposed—more on this below). At first a USA might be small and have meager returns, particularly those of people from poor families, but over time regular deposits by the worker and his or her employer(s) and perhaps contributions by the government or other sources would help it grow. Eventually there would be enough for a down payment on a house, establishing geographic rootedness and building another form of equity. Alternatively, or perhaps after rebuilding the account, the account holder might use funds to invest in education and training as tools for greater productivity and increased income. At times of unemployment the holder could draw or borrow from the account until finding a new job. Over a working life, through contributions, tax savings, and returns on investments, the assets in the account should accumulate to the point of allowing one to retire. After death, the assets would pass on to the account holder's heirs, helping them to establish their own USAs. Funds could even be transferable before death to a dependent's USA, if the holder so chooses. In sum, such a multiple purpose asset-building account could function very much in the way the land had once functioned in American life.

Radical policy changes would not be needed to make this vision a reality for most citizens, that is, the middle class and the well-to-do. Public policy would have to keep moving, as it has been, towards creating tax deductions, deferrals, and exemptions for contributions to, earnings on, and withdrawals from special purpose individual savings and investment accounts. Businesses would have to move not only towards defined-contribution retirement accounts, as many have been, but also towards making these accounts more portable for employees who leave the company. These trends could, without much difficulty, converge into something like USAs as described above. The more formidable challenge is to open the door for participation by the poor. The IDA concept is one key to that door. Tax deductions, deferrals and exemptions are of little use to poor people who don't pay much in income taxes, but IDA-like cocontributions by government or nonprofit agencies could help such people get an asset-building account off the ground. As indicated above, I think IDAs are very promising, but they also have limitations, two of which in particular stand out.

First, individual investment accounts will not, of themselves, solve the problem of poverty. Whenever or wherever unemployment is high or wages are low, there will be poverty; these factors are fundamental. IDAs cannot replace the need for job opportunities, nor, despite the animus of the republican tradition, for income support programs in the absence of such opportunities. IDAs can fund education and training, which will help many people find jobs or get better jobs, or can help some others create their own jobs as microentrepreneurs, but otherwise IDAs will have minimal effect on employment or income. Of course, eliminating poverty is too high a goal for any single policy; IDAs could still improve lives and perhaps change behaviors and attitudes in desirable ways. I would also like to make it clear that I am not arguing that unemployment or low incomes are necessarily a barrier to establishing IDAs, that people on welfare or in low-wage jobs could never afford to save anything and therefore could not make deposits in an IDA.[7] To the contrary, there have always been poor people who have found ways to save; thus it is quite plausible that there are other factors besides income level that affect saving, including the institutional vehicles of savings available.[8] Creating a small savings account that earns a pitiful rate of interest and disqualifies its owner from welfare benefits, if those should become needed, may not be worth the sacrifice. But an IDA, which would more quickly build a nest egg for the further development of assets, could be a real incentive to save and a more fitting reward to those who make such extraordinary sacrifices to improve their lives.

The second limitation is that as a bridge to USAs, IDAs end somewhere in the middle of the river. To have an IDA become a USA, as described above, would require a continual building of an account over the holder's working life. As currently structured, cocontributions to an IDA cease when a certain amount is reached, and the account is closed when the funds are spent for the designated purpose. Once the holder puts a down payment on a house, or pays tuition, or starts up a small business, their participation in the IDA program is finished. Unless the holder was able to rebuild an account through savings alone, without the cocontributions, there would be no funds available for other asset-building purposes. In contrast, the kind of USA I described above would fund multiple purposes, not just one, continually rebuilding its funds through regular deposits, tax savings, and returns on investments. Of course, we can imagine continuing cocontributions for those whose incomes remain too low to contribute much to their investment accounts; it is obvious that the primary obstacle is, at bottom, finding the money. Any large scale program of long-term IDAs would be very expensive. Sherraden gives a ballpark estimate of nearly $19 billion annually for a program of multi-purpose IDAs for the poor,[9] which is higher than the annual federal budget for the Temporary Assistance for Needy Families program (formerly Aid to Families with Dependent Children). In addition, there are many families whose income exceeds the official poverty line but who are, by most standards, still poor; to include any of these families in an IDA program would increase the cost even more.

Cocontributions for the IDAs currently in existence have been funded primarily from private sources such as foundations, corporations, and nonprofit organizations. If IDAs prove to have the positive effects anticipated, it is likely that even more such money will become available. But it is hard to imagine that private sources alone will produce sufficient funds for a large-scale IDA program; proponents therefore have sought public money. Although a bipartisan coalition formed to support a multimillion dollar IDA demonstration program funded by federal dollars,[10] political support for a more comprehensive program is likely to be much more difficult to gain. The prospect of transferring billions of dollars of public funds into bank accounts for poor people would undoubtedly be controversial, and likely to be attacked as a redistribution of wealth. Opposition based on these grounds would be even more likely if the expense were to be offset by reducing tax subsidies for higher income households, as Sherraden has proposed.[11] Redistribution has never been a popular idea in the United States; the republican tradition was called upon to guide the initial distribution of the public lands, not to justify redistributing land that was already privately owned.

President Clinton's Universal Savings Account proposal, first raised in his 1999 State of the Union address (a similar proposal was briefly mentioned in his 2000 State of the Union Address), is conceptually similar to IDAs but relies on tax credits, which are generally more politically acceptable than direct grant programs. Unlike tax deductions and exemptions, tax credits are often refundable (the tax filer receives money back if the credit is larger than the tax owed) and low-income tax filers can thus get full value from them. The President's plan would give a tax credit (larger for lower income households) for an initial deposit into a special retirement account, and a tax credit (again scaled in reverse size to income) for additional contributions up to an annual maximum. The proposal is aimed at aiding low-to-middle income households save for retirement, and is estimated to cost about $38 billion a year or more.[12] These funds would come from anticipated federal revenue surpluses, for which, of course, competing claims have been made. Whether his USA proposal will be more attractive than these other claims, assuming the predicted surpluses actually materialize, is yet to be tested.

Are there other ways to help the poor build long-term savings and investment accounts on a widespread scale? An employer mandate is another possibility. All employers, including those who employ low wage, part-time and temporary employees, could be compelled to contribute to their employees' accounts, perhaps matching an employee's voluntary payroll deduction of regular deposits. This is probably no more feasible politically than large-scale public funding, but a very similar idea may be more salable. Employers and employees already contribute equal shares to the Social Security retirement system via a payroll tax. There are several proposals currently in play to fully or partially privatize the Social Security "trust fund" (actually an accounting device and not a real trust fund), moving some or all of the payroll taxes collected into individual investment accounts of some kind. If some portion of the payroll tax were diverted into something like a USA, with the remainder continuing to fund a defined benefit safety net for retirees (vital for people who end up retiring during prolonged downturns in investment markets), the regular contributions and returns on investments over a working life could help to build up accounts for the working poor. The catch is that any diversion of the Social Security payroll tax will exacerbate the long-term financing problem of the Social Security system. President Clinton's USA proposal was developed specifically to counter the diversion of Social Security revenues into individual investment accounts.

4. CONSIDERING KELSO'S POLICY IDEAS

A final possibility for funding investment accounts for the poor is Louis Kelso's proposal to use credit.[13] Practical experience with leveraged

Employee Stock Ownership Plans has demonstrated that making new stockholders through credit is at least feasible,[14] but consideration of Kelso's larger policy program has run into two obstacles. One is that of determining the relation between Kelso's practical policy program and controversial aspects of his economic theory. There are two schools of thought on this issue. There are those who argue that his policy program is necessarily grounded in his theory, and thus that they stand and fall together; some argue that they stand together, and others that they fall together. On the other hand, there are those that believe the theory and the practical proposals are separable. Kelso's economic theory is founded on concepts that radically challenge conventional schools of economics, and the disputes it has provoked are impossible to sort through in a brief space. In my judgment, at least some of his practical program is separable from his theory; the institution of ESOPs is evidence of this. But I do not want to imply that his theory ought therefore to be set aside and ignored. It is unfortunate that thorough and careful published analyses are very hard to find.[15] In my view, the theory is interesting and in some respects plausible enough to warrant further study and refinement, and I find some of the most common criticisms of it to be misplaced.[16]

The second obstacle to considering Kelso's (non-ESOP) policy ideas is that they are usually presented as a very large-scale program; that is, as a comprehensive program to make all citizens owners of significant capital estates. Indeed, the vision of citizen-capitalists Kelso was trying to advance in *The Capitalist Manifesto* nearly a half a century ago goes even beyond that of a nation in which all citizens own their own USA. If Kelso's claims are to be believed, his Financed Capitalist Plan (FCP) would overcome the limitations of IDAs noted above, allowing the capital-poor to become capital owners without recourse to redistribution, supplementing low wages with capital incomes, and triggering steady economic growth. Such broad-ranging claims understandably provoke caution, if not skepticism. More specifically, a large-scale program would require a significant expansion of credit to fund new capital investments by the "new capitalists." Because arguments about whether or not this would be inflationary necessarily rely on economic theory, they often lead back into the arguments about Kelso's theory.

At this point, I would recommend implementing policy based on Kelso's ideas selectively and incrementally, allowing time to study, perfect, expand, or discard them with experience. If they prove to work as well as ESOPs have, this should give impetus to consideration of a broader program. The problem of poverty is both pressing and puzzling, puzzling because of its continued existence in the midst of astounding productive capacity. Even allowing for exaggeration in Kelso's claims for his larger program, it is worth experimenting to determine if there is any potential there for helping to solve the puzzle of poverty in the modern world.

5. Sketch of a Policy Program

Based on the analysis above, I will sketch out a simple set of suggestions for building a postindustrial civic republican policy program. I have three principal suggestions, which build one upon the other: (1) consolidate existing individual investment accounts, (2) expand cocontributions for the poor, and (3) experiment with the use of credit to make new capital owners.

Consolidate existing individual investment accounts.

Currently there are a multitude of individual and work-related investment account options, including traditional IRAs (deductible and nondeductible), Roth IRAs, educational savings accounts, 401(k)s, 403(b)s, Keoghs, IDAs, and so on, all with different rules, and yet even more variations are being proposed. As financial writer Jane Bryant Quinn has said:

> I'm more persuaded by Roth's idea of reviving the universal IRA—a tax-deductible, tax-deferred plan that anyone could use. Maybe it could be one, simple vessel, open to contributions from workers, employers and the government, too. Maybe there could be two investment tracks—one with plenty of choice for people with large sums of money, one with two low-cost choices (stock fund or bond fund) for small accounts. . . . People can be paralyzed by too many choices. Make it simple, sweetie, and watch the savings pile up.[17]

Low- and moderate-income citizens are the most likely to be frightened off by a bewildering array of complicated options. The aim should be to simplify the choices by converting all of these into one or two multiple-purpose individual investment accounts along the lines of the USAs I described above. These accounts would be portable from job to job, tax-protected, dedicated to asset-building purposes, usable in emergencies such as unemployment, and inheritable. Deposits could come from the account holders, employer contributions, and other sources.

Expand cocontributions for the poor.

Building on the current experiments with IDAs and any lessons learned about how to design them most successfully, IDA-type parallel accounts to the USAs of poor people should be offered by state and local governments, nonprofit organizations, and businesses employing low-wage workers. The federal government should facilitate these efforts with tax incentives, help with administrative costs, and perhaps additional funds for the cocontributions on some kind of matching basis. A national effort to publicize IDAs and encourage charitable donations and business participation should be undertaken in order to draw in as many different sources of funding as possible.

The design of these IDAs should aim at longer-term goals than they presently do. Currently an IDA is terminated once the account holder achieves one specific goal (buying a house, starting a microenterprise, or paying for education). Instead, the aim should be to build the account holder's total assets (the IDA and USA, home and business equity, educational level, and any other assets) to a certain level while providing a means for the account holder to demonstrate financial responsibility. Once this level is achieved and responsibility has been demonstrated, any funds remaining in the IDA would be transferred to the account holder's USA and the parallel account terminated.

Experiment with the use of credit.

To help with the funding problem, the possibilities for using credit to create new capital owners should be thoroughly explored. For example, ESOP-like trust funds with low-asset households rather than employees as beneficiaries could be created; once a trust fund repays its obligations the equities in the fund could be transferred to the beneficiaries' USAs (or IDAs). Variations of Kelso's basic idea have been developed by different writers,[18] but unfortunately very few academic, foundation, or public resources have been dedicated to examining or testing these proposals. Much more research and experimentation on Kelso's ideas should be undertaken.

Whatever the structure of any credit-based program is otherwise, it should insure that there is a link between being a beneficiary and demonstrating civic virtues. In addition to income and asset tests, qualifications should include evidence of good character, for example, that the applicant finish high school, be free of felony convictions, and have a reasonably stable work history. Financial responsibility (e.g., saving for asset-building goals) could also be demonstrated through participation in an IDA program.

6. CONCLUSION

The research presented in this book has shown the continued influence of the civic republican tradition on U.S. poverty policy. Changing economic conditions created problems of coherency for the application of this tradition to poverty policy in the twentieth century. This final chapter summed up these problems and sketched out a policy program that could aid the poor in a way compatible with a more coherent modern version of the civic republican tradition.

Notes

Notes to Chapter 1:
Introduction: Policy Analysis
and Ethical Traditions

1. William A. Gamson and Andre Modigliani, "The Changing Culture of Affirmative Action," in *Research in Political Sociology*, ed. Richard D. Braungart (Greenwich, CT: JAI Press, 1987), v. 3: 143.

2. The typical case was the Family Support Act of 1988, a reform of the Aid to Families with Dependent Children program (see ch. 4). The anomalous case was the Home Ownership and Opportunity for People Everywhere program, which was backed by an unusual alliance of conservative Republicans and black Democrats (see ch. 3).

3. I also added a third case on plans for broadening asset ownership which fit the developing theme of the research (ch. 5).

4. For a wide-ranging discussion of these trends, see Frank Fischer and John Forester, eds., *The Argumentative Turn in Policy Analysis and Planning* (Durham, NC: Duke Univ. Press, 1993).

5 . Murray Edelman, *The Symbolic Uses of Politics* (Chicago: Univ. of Chicago Press, 1964); Edelman, *Politics As Symbolic Action* (Chicago: Markham Publishing Co., 1971); Edelman, *Political Language* (New York: Academic Press, 1977).

6. Roger W. Cobb and Charles D. Elder, *Participation in American Politics* (Boston: Allyn and Bacon, Inc., 1972); Elder and Cobb, *The Political Uses of Symbols* (New York: Longman, 1983).

7. William A. Gamson and Kathryn E. Lasch, "The Political Culture of Social Welfare Policy," in *Evaluating the Welfare State*, ed. Shimon E. Spiro and Ephraim Yuchtman-Yaar, ch. 22 (New York: Academic Press, 1983); Gamson and Modigliani, "Changing Culture of Affirmative Action."

8. John W. Kingdon, *Agendas, Alternatives, and Public Policies* (New York: Harper-Collins, 1984, 1995).

9. Kingdon, *Agendas, Alternatives, and Public Policies*, 116, 140–45.

10. Janet A. Weiss, "The Powers of Problem Definition: The Case of Government Paperwork," *Policy Sciences* 22 (May 1989): 97–121; David A. Rochefort and Roger W. Cobb, eds., *The Politics of Problem Definition* (Lawrence, KA: Univ. Press of Kansas, 1994).

11. Paul A. Sabatier and Hank C. Jenkins-Smith, eds., *Policy Change and Learning* (Boulder, CO: Westview Press, 1993); Frank R. Baumgartner and Bryan D. Jones, *Agendas and Instability in American Politics* (Chicago: Univ. of Chicago Press, 1993).

12. Malcolm B. Hamilton surveyed the various "idea elements" attached to the term and weighed the usefulness of each for empirical research; his proposed definition is similar to the one I offer here. Hamilton, "The Elements of the Concept of Ideology," *Political Studies* 35 (March 1987): 18–38.

13. Aristotle, *The Politics:* bk. 3, chs. 8–9; bk. 5, ch. 1; bk. 6, ch. 3.

14. My presentation of the history of the concept of ideology draws from other authors' interpretations, principally: George Lichtheim, "The Concept of Ideology," in *The Concept of Ideology and Other Essays* (New York: Random House, 1967), 1: 3–46; Mostafa Rejai, "Ideology," in *Dictionary of the History of Ideas*, ed. Philip P. Wiener (New York: Charles Scribner's Sons, 1973), 552–59; David McLellan, *Ideology* (Milton Keynes, England: Open Univ. Press, 1986), chs. 1–4; John G. Gunnell, *The Descent of Political Theory* (Chicago: Univ. of Chicago Press, 1993), ch. 7; and Lynn McDonald, *The Early Origins of the Social Sciences* (Montreal and Kingston: McGill-Queen's Univ. Press, 1993), ch. 6.

For a sampling of the work of key theorists, see Karl Marx, "The German Ideology, Part I," in *The Marx-Engels Reader*, ed. Richard C. Tucker (New York: W. W. Norton and Co., 1978), 147–200; Max Weber, "Protestant Asceticism and the Spirit of Capitalism" (selection from *The Protestant Ethic and the "Spirit" of Capitalism*) and "Value-judgments in Social Science" in *Max Weber: Selections in Translation*, ed. W. G. Runciman (Cambridge: Cambridge Univ. Press, 1978), 138–73, 69–98; and Karl Mannheim, *Ideology and Utopia* (New York: Harcourt, Brace and World, Inc., 1968).

15. Mannheim, *Ideology and Utopia*, 84–96, 253–56, 269–71. I use the term ideology broadly to cover what Mannheim distinguishes as "ideologies" and "utopias."

16. Mannheim, *Ideology and Utopia*, 130–46.

17. Charles Beard, *An Economic Interpretation of the Constitution of the United States* (New York: Macmillan, 1913). Beard was a progressive rather than a Marxist, although the Marxist influence on his scholarly work is apparent; see Gunnell, *Descent of Political Theory*, 84–86; and Raymond Seidelman with Edward J. Harpham, *Disenchanted Realists* (Albany: State Univ. of New York Press, 1985), 81–97.

18. Lasswell's published work is voluminous, extending over a long career; for an overview of his work see Seidelman, *Disenchanted Realists*, 133–45, and Gunnell, *Descent of Political Theory*, 121–25. A succinct treatment of political symbols may be found in Harold D. Lasswell and Abraham Kaplan, *Power and Society* (New Haven, CT: Yale Univ. Press, 1950), ch. 6.

19. Gunnell, *Descent of Political Theory*, chs. 6: 8–11; McLellan, *Ideology*, ch. 5.

20. The best known version of this argument is Daniel Bell, *The End of Ideology* (Cambridge, MA: Harvard Univ. Press, 1988), originally published in 1960.

21. A couple of the early classics are David B. Truman, *The Governmental Process* (New York: Alfred A. Knopf, 1951); and Anthony Downs, *An Economic Theory of Democracy* (New York: Harper, 1957).

22. For a recent collection of such criticisms, see Jane J. Mansbridge, *Beyond Self-Interest* (Chicago: Univ. of Chicago Press, 1990).

23. I am presenting a version of such a critique myself. It shows itself above, in my historical interpretation of the development of different theoretical positions in American political science as a response to political conditions, and in section 4 below, in my argument that utilitarian moral theory has dominated research agendas.

24. John W. Kingdon, "Politicians, Self-Interest, and Ideas," in *Reconsidering the Democratic Public*, ed. George E. Marcus and Russell L. Hanson, ch. 3 (University Park: The Pennsylvania State Univ. Press, 1993).

25. Clifford Geertz, "Ideology as a Cultural System," in *Ideology and Discontent*, ed. David E. Apter (New York: The Free Press of Glencoe, 1964), 1: 59 & 61. According to Geertz, the chief difference between science and ideology is one of stylistic strategy.

26. Positivism is one type of objectivist theory, which regards valid knowledge as empirically tested knowledge of the properties and relations of natural phenomena.

27. Lawrence Tribe, "Policy Studies: Analysis or Ideology," *Philosophy and Public Affairs* 2 (Fall 1972): 66–110; David Dery, *Problem Definition in Policy Analysis* (Lawrence, KA: Univ. Press of Kansas, 1984); M. E. Hawkesworth, *Theoretical Issues in Policy Analysis* (Albany: State Univ. of New York Press, 1988); and Deborah Stone, *Policy Paradox* (New York: W. W . Norton and Company, 1988, 1997).

28. Policy analysts have also used a social cost / benefit analysis as a substitute for political processes to determine which policies would best satisfy citizens' aggregated preferences. The analyst measures and weighs citizens' preferences concerning a particular policy option by estimating market prices for the goods affected by the policy. This method is conceptually based on utilitarianism (see the next paragraph of the text), and has serious problems handling the distribution of costs and benefit among individuals. Distributional issues, of course, are often at the very heart of policy disputes. On the grounding of cost / benefit analysis in utilitarianism, see Hank C. Jenkins-Smith, *Democratic Politics and Policy Analysis* (Pacific Grove, CA: Brooks / Cole Publishing Company, 1990).

29. 1 will avoid the issue of whether the natural sciences differ from the social sciences in this respect with the traditional waiver: it is outside the scope of this study.

30. The concept of research paradigms that become defeated by a gradual collection of anomalies comes from Thomas S. Kuhn, *The Structure of Scientific Revolutions* (Chicago: Univ. of Chicago Press, 1970).

31. Robert S. Erikson and Norman Luttbeg, *American Public Opinion* (New York: John Wiley and Sons, Inc., 1973), ch. 2; Donald R. Kinder, "Diversity and Complexity in American Public Opinion," in *Political Science: The State of the Discipline*, ed. Ada Finifter, ch. 3 (Washington, DC: The American Political Science Association, 1983).

32. Peter O. Steiner, "The Public Sector and the Public Interest," *Public Expenditure and Policy Analysis*, ed. Robert H. Haveman and Julius Margolis (Chicago: Rand McNally, 1977), 13–45; David O. Sears, Richard R. Lau, Tom R. Tyler, and Harris M. Allen, Jr., "Self-Interest vs. Symbolic Politics in Policy Attitudes and Presidential Voting," *American Political Science Review* 74 (Sept. 1980): 670–84.

33. Two good examples of research based on such an agenda are Steven Kelman, *Making Public Policy* (New York: Basic Books, Inc., Publishers, 1987); and Daniel Yankelovich, *Coming to Public Judgment* (Syracuse, NY: Syracuse Univ. Press, 1993).

34. Think of Kingdon's policy entrepreneur (section 1, "Policy Frames in Policy Studies") trying to link problem, policy, and politics.

35. See section 4, "The Non-separability of Facts and Values in Social Research."

36. David Hume, *A Treatise of Human Nature* (1740).

37. Jeremy Bentham, *An Introduction to the Principles of Morals and Legislation* (1789, 1823).

38. Welfare economics accepts the satisfaction of individual preferences as an aim and searches for institutions that can best accomplish this. Markets are in most instances considered the most efficient mechanism, but governments have a role in those special situations where markets are inadequate for one reason or another. Public policy, therefore, is justified when it helps maximize the satisfaction of the individual preferences of citizens. Charles A. Lave and James G. March, *An Introduction to Models in the Social Sciences* (New York: Harper and Row, 1975), ch. 5; Edwin Mansfield, *Micro-Economics, Selected Readings* (New York: Norton, 1985), 3: 8–11; Richard A. Musgrave and Peggy B. Musgrave, *Public Finance in Theory and Practice* (New York: McGraw-Hill, 1976), ch. 3.

39. Alasdair MacIntyre, *Whose Justice? Which Rationality?* (London: Duckworth, 1988); see also: MacIntyre, *Three Rival Versions of Moral Inquiry* (London: Duckworth, 1990).

40. Martin Rein, "Value-Critical Policy Analysis," in *Ethics, the Social Sciences, and Policy Analysis*, ed. Daniel Callahan and Bruce Jennings (New York: Plenum Press, 1983), 88–109.

41. Rein, *From Policy to Practice* (Armonk, NY: M. E. Sharpe, Inc., 1983); Donald A. Schön and Rein, *Frame Reflection* (New York: BasicBooks, 1994).

42. In Rein and Schön's terms, I have focused on a "rhetorical frame," which is found in the language used to discuss policy before the public, rather than an "action frame," which influences the actual form of laws, regulations, and so forth (Rein and Schön, *Frame Reflection*, 32–36). This is a useful distinction, but in this case, at least, I think the rhetorical frame has set real parameters for the political survival of any action frame.

43. Frank Fischer, *Evaluating Public Policy* (Chicago: Nelson-Hall, 1995).

44. Ibid., 71, 75–81.

45. Ibid., xi.

Notes to Chapter 2:
Dependence and Independence
in the Nineteenth Century

1. Gordon S. Wood, *The Radicalism of the American Revolution* (New York: Alfred A. Knopf, 1992), 18–33.

2. Wood, *Radicalism*, 33–38; Gaston V. Rimlinger, *Welfare Policy and Industrialization in Europe, America, and Russia* (New York: John Wiley and Sons, Inc., 1971), 16–17.

3. Walter I. Trattner, *From Poor Law to Welfare State* (New York: the Free Press, 1984), 4–12; James Leiby, *A History of Social Welfare and Social Work in the United States* (New York: Columbia Univ. Press, 1978), 38–40; June Axinn and Herman Levin, *Social Welfare*, 3rd ed. (New York: Longman, 1992), 13–14.

4. William B. Scott, *In Pursuit of Happiness* (Bloomington, IN: Indiana Univ. Press, 1977), 14–15; Wood, *Radicalism*, 122–123; Allan Kulikoff, *The Agrarian Origins of American Capitalism* (Charlottesville, VA: Univ. Press of Virginia, 1992), 66.

5. David J. Rothman, *The Discovery of the Asylum* (Boston: Little, Brown and Co., 1990), chs. 1–2; Trattner, *From Poor Law*, 23–24; Axinn and Levin, *Social Welfare*, 17–19.

6. Wood, *Radicalism*, 53–58, 112–120.

7. Scott, *In Pursuit*, 1–14; Kulikoff, *Agrarian Origins*, 39–41.

8. Kulikoff, *Agrarian Origins*, 130–132.

9. Scott, *In Pursuit*, 2–3.

10. Ibid., 15–23. The most such attacks achieved were discriminatory taxes on such unused landholdings, but not confiscation or direct redistribution.

11. The extent of Locke's influence, relative to other currents of political thought in the colonies, has not gone unquestioned. See note 15.

12. H. F. Russell Smith, *Harrington and His Oceana* (Cambridge: Cambridge Univ. Press, 1914); J. G. A. Pocock, "The History of the Ideology: Harrington's Ideas After His Lifetime," in James Harrington, *The Political Works of James Harrington*, ed. Pocock, ch. 7 (Cambridge, ENG: Cambridge Univ. Press, 1977).

13. Harrington outlined a complex system in which an elected senate would propose questions and the people would resolve them; it featured secret ballots, indirect elections for some offices, and separation of powers. He regarded rotation of officeholders and "the agrarian" (his property laws) to be fundamental. His presentation of electoral devices is widely considered to have had some influence on the creation of American institutions,

but it was his theory of the relation of property ownership to political stability that was his original contribution to political theory.

14. Harrington's "Thirteenth Order" of Oceana specifies the agrarian law; *Political Works*, 231.

15. Wood, *Radicalism*, 95–110, 174–179; Bernard Bailyn, *The Ideological Origins of the American Revolution* (Cambridge, MA: Belnap Press, 1967); Lance Banning, *The Jeffersonian Persuasion* (Ithaca, NY: Cornell Univ. Press, 1978), 42–83. The literature on the political ideas prevailing at the time of the founding not only has a long history, but it has exploded over the last few decades. Central issues have been whether to characterize colonial ideas as reflecting multiple conflicting traditions or broad ideological consensus, and, if the latter, whether it was dominated by classical republicanism or Lockean liberalism. My more limited aim is to trace the development of an important tradition in American political language, not to characterize American ideas as a whole. For a fine review of this literature, see: Daniel T. Rodgers, "Republicanism: The Career of a Concept," *Journal of American History* 79 (June 1992).

16. Wood, *Radicalism*, 125–135, 170–173; Joyce Appleby, *Liberalism and Republicanism in the Historical Imagination* (Cambridge, MA: Harvard Univ. Press, 1992), ch. 5.

17. Kulikoff, *Agrarian Origins*, 132–136.

18. Ibid., 69–70.

19. Ibid., 136–146; Wood, *Radicalism*, 184–187; Bailyn, *Ideological Origins*, ch. 6, sec. 1; Patrice Higonnet, *Sister Republics* (Cambridge, MA: Harvard Univ. Press, 1988), 183–184.

20. Robert E. Shalhope, *The Roots of Democracy* (Boston: Twayne Publishers, 1990), 132–137. Of course, one of the main reasons that slavery persisted (even as indentured servitude was abandoned) was that the economic incentives in favor of slavery were greatly increased with the invention of the cotton gin in 1793.

21. Drew R. McCoy, *The Elusive Republic* (Chapel Hill: Univ. of North Carolina Press, 1980), particularly 12–16, 48–75; Scott, *In Pursuit*, 53–58.

22. Scott, *In Pursuit*, 41.

23. Noble E. Cunningham, Jr., *In Pursuit of Reason* (Baton Rouge: Louisiana State Univ. Press, 1987), 55–56; Appleby, *Liberalism and Republicanism*, 300–301. Entail is inheritance through the stem line of a family; primogeniture is inheritance by the eldest son. Both devices were intended to keep large estates intact, as opposed to dividing them among the deceased's survivors.

24. Wood, *Radicalism*, 183.

25. I am using the word "agrarian" to refer to a preference for an economy based primarily on agriculture; the "agrarian republicans" desired a society dominated by numerous independent, property-owning farmers. I am not using "agrarian" in the sense which it was often used in the nineteenth century, as a pejorative meant to associate people with radical proposals for the redistribution of land. Nor do I mean to imply a backward-looking mentality opposed to economic development, which is how Jeffersonians have sometimes been characterized by modern writers; Appleby, *Liberalism and Republicanism*, ch. 10 is an excellent discussion of the practical basis and forward-looking character of the Jeffersonian program.

26. On the development of these opposing economic positions, see McCoy, *Elusive Republic*, chs. 4–6. On the public land question specifically, see Murray R. Benedict, *Farm Policies of the United States 1790–1950* (New York: The Twentieth Century Fund, 1953), 4–5; Roy M. Robbins, *Our Landed Heritage*, 2nd ed. (Lincoln: Univ. of Nebraska Press, 1976), 13–15; and Benjamin Horace Hibbard, *A History of the Public Land Policies* (New York: The MacMillan Co., 1924), 2–4. Cathy D. Matson and Peter S. Onuf, *A Union of Interests* (Lawrence: Univ. Press of Kansas, 1990), make a persuasive argument that the proponents of the new Constitution succeeded by linking the proposed new government to the aim of national economic development.

27. Robbins, *Our Landed Heritage*, 7–13; Benedict, *Farm Policies*, 10–13; Daniel Feller, *The Public Lands in Jacksonian Politics* (Madison, WI: Univ. of Wisconsin Press, 1984), 6–7; Hibbard, *History of the Public Land Policies*, 32–60.

28. Representative Scott, *Annals of Congress*, 1st Cong., 1st sess., 13 July 1789, 650. (There are two editions of the 1st Congress' *Annals*, almost exactly identical but having different paginations. I have given the page number for the edition that was available to me.)

29. For a summary of the debate, see Hibbard, *History of the Public Land Policies*, 60–67.

30. Representative Holland, *Annals of Congress*, 4th Cong., 1st sess., 5 April 1796, 858–59.

31. Representative Crabb, Ibid., 860.

32. Benedict, *Farm Policies*, 13–14; Robbins, *Our Landed Heritage*, 15–19; Hibbard, *History of the Public Land Policies*, 67–71.

33. McCoy, *Elusive Republic*, 185–188; Banning, *Jeffersonian Persuasion*, chs. 5–9; Kulikoff, *Agrarian Origins*, 146–151. See also the exchanges between Banning and Appleby: Lance Banning, "Jeffersonian Ideology Revisited: Liberal and Classical Ideas in the New American Republic," *William & Mary Quarterly* 43 (Jan. 1986): 3–19; Appleby, *Liberalism and Republicanism*, chs. 12–13.

34. McCoy, *Elusive Republic*, 196–259.

35. Feller, *Public Lands in Jacksonian Politics*, 10, 13–16; Robbins, *Our Landed Heritage*, 28–29.

36. Feller, *Public Lands in Jacksonian Politics*, 18–27; Robbins, *Our Landed Heritage*, 29–34; Hibbard, *History of the Public Land Policies*, 97–98.

37. Feller, *Public Lands in Jacksonian Politics*, 27–31.

38. Feller, *Public Lands in Jacksonian Politics*, 68–159; Scott, *In Pursuit*, 58–60; Robbins, *Our Landed Heritage*, 35–58.

39. *Register of Debates in Congress*, 19th Cong., 1st sess., 16 May 1826, 727–728.

40. "4th Annual Message to Congress" (4 Dec. 1832), in *A Compilation of the Messages and Papers of the Presidents, 1789–1897*, ed. James D. Richardson, vol. II (Washington, DC: U.S. Government Printing Office, 1896–1899), 600–601.

41. Marvin Meyers, *The Jacksonian Persuasion* (Stanford, CA: Stanford Univ. Press, 1960), 20–24; Merrill D. Peterson, ed., *Democracy, Liberty and Property* (Indianapolis, IN: Bobbs-Merrill Co., Inc., 1966), 135–137, 187–214, 279–281, 377–409; Scott, *In Pursuit*, 75–79.

42. Chancellor Kent, quoted in Peterson, *Democracy, Liberty and Property*, 193–194.

43. "Memorial of the Non-Freeholders of the City of Richmond," quoted in Peterson, *Democracy, Liberty and Property*, 382.

44. Peterson, *Democracy, Liberty and Property*, 59–67, 137–138, 194–196, 214–233, 346, 401–402.

45. McCoy, *Elusive Republic*, 49–61, 105–112.

46. Ibid., 113–119.

47. Scott, *In Pursuit*, 73–74, 87–93; Jean Matthews, *Toward a New Society* (Boston: Twayne Publishers, 1991), 142; Peterson, *Democracy, Liberty and Property*, 203.

48. Michael B. Katz, *In the Shadow of the Poorhouse* (New York: Basic Books, 1986), 4–10.

49. Meyers, *Jacksonian Persuasion*, 122–128; Wood, *Radicalism*, 276–286.

50. Rothman, *Discovery of the Asylum;* Katz, *Shadow of the Poorhouse*, 10–13; Leiby, *History of Social Welfare*, 48–70; Matthews, *Toward a New Society*, 144–148.

51. "The Josiah Quincy Report of 1821 on the Pauper Laws of Massachusetts," *Public Welfare Administration in the United States: Select Documents*, ed. Sophonisba P. Breckinridge, 2nd ed. (Chicago: Univ. of Chicago Press, 1938), 34.

52. Rothman, *Discovery of the Asylum*, chs. 7–8; Katz, *Shadow of the Poorhouse*, 13–25; Trattner, *Poor Law to Welfare State*, 52–59.

53. Katz, *Shadow of the Poorhouse*, ch. 2; Josephine Chapin Brown, *Public Relief 1929–1939* (New York: Henry Holt and Co., 1940), 39–46.

54. Robbins, *Our Landed Heritage*, 96–116; Scott, *In Pursuit*, 60–67; Hibbard, *History of the Public Land Policies*, 356–373; George M. Stephenson, *The Political History of the Public Lands from 1840 to 1862* (New York: Russell and Russell, 1917, 1967), 103–117, 132–148.

55. Mary E. Young, "Congress Looks West: Liberal Ideology and Public Land Policy in the Nineteenth Century," in *The Frontier in American Development*, ed. David M. Ellis (Ithaca, NY: Cornell Univ. Press, 1969), 74–112.

56. Representative Cable, *Congressional Globe*, 32nd Cong., 1st sess., Appendix, 10 March 1852, 298.

57. Senator Johnson, *Congressional Globe*, 36th Cong., 1st sess., 12 April 1860, 1653.

58. Robbins, *Our Landed Heritage*, 174–178; Stephenson, *Political History of the Public Lands*, 149–193.

59. Eric Foner, *Free Soil, Free Labor, Free Men* (New York: Oxford Univ. Press, 1970), 11–18, 23–31, 40–51.

60. Foner, *Free Soil*, 24–29.

61. Robbins, *Our Landed Heritage*, 178–182, 203–207; Scott, *In Pursuit*, 67–69; Hibbard, *History of the Public Land Policies*, 373–385; Stephenson, *Political History of the Public Lands*, 193–245.

62. Quoted in Robbins, *Our Landed Heritage*, 206.

63. Robbins, *Our Landed Heritage*, 210–213; Michael L. Lanza, *Agrarianism and Reconstruction Politics* (Baton Rouge, LA: Louisiana State Univ. Press, 1990).

64. Robbins, *Our Landed Heritage*, 236.

65. Robbins, *Our Landed Heritage*, 240; Lanza, *Agrarianism and Reconstruction*, 57–71, 79–85, 105–111.

66. Robbins, *Our Landed Heritage*, 223–224.

67. Ibid., 271–276.

68. Foner, *Free Soil*, 32–33; Scott, *In Pursuit*, 70; Fred A. Shannon, "The Homestead Act and the Labor Surplus," in *The Public Lands*, ed. Vernon Carstensen (Madison, WI: Univ. of Wisconsin Press, 1963), 304–308.

69. Stanford J. Layton, *To No Privileged Class* (Salt Lake City, UT: Charles Reed Center for Western Studies, Brigham Young Univ., 1988).

70. Franklin D. Roosevelt, "Back to the Land," *Review of Reviews* (Oct. 1931); Donald Holley, *Uncle Sam's Farmers* (Urbana, IL: Univ. of Illinois Press, 1975), 20–23.

71. Diane Ghirardo, *Building New Communities* (Princeton, NJ: Princeton Univ. Press, 1989).

72. Paul E. Mertz, *New Deal Policy and Southern Rural Poverty* (Baton Rouge, LA: Louisiana State Univ. Press, 1978).

73. *Public Papers and Addresses of Franklin D. Roosevelt*, ed. Samuel I. Rosenman (New York: Random House, 1938), 5: 438–39.

74. Sidney Baldwin, *Poverty and Politics* (Chapel Hill, NC: Univ. of North Carolina Press, 1968).

Notes to Chapter 3:
Homeownership for the Poor

1. See section 6, "A Legacy of Political Language" in ch. 2.

2. Jan Cohn, *The Palace or the Poorhouse* (E. Lansing, MI: Michigan State Univ. Press, 1979).

3. Pearl Janet Davies, *Real Estate in American History* (Washington, DC: Public Affairs Press, 1958), 49.

4. Davies, *Real Estate*, 137–140.

5. Diane Ghirardo, *Building New Communities* (Princeton, NJ: Princeton Univ. Press, 1989), 14.

6. Cohn, *Palace or Poorhouse*, 238, citing *Home Ownership, Income and Types of Dwellings*, vol. IV of *The Reports of the President's Conference on Home Building and Home Ownership*, 2, 30.

7. "Address to the White House Conference on Home Building and Home Ownership" (2 Dec. 1931), in *Public Papers of the Presidents of the United States: Herbert Hoover, 1931* (Washington, DC: U.S. Government Printing Office, 1976), 573.

8. George Sternlieb and David Listokin, "A Review of National Housing Policy," in *Housing America's Poor,* ed. Peter D. Salins (Chapel Hill, NC: Univ. of North Carolina Press, 1987), 2: 18–19; Glenn H. Beyer, *Housing and Society* (New York: The MacMillan Co., 1965), 250.

9. J. Paul Mitchell, ed., *Federal Housing Policy and Programs* (NJ: Center for Urban Policy Research, Rutgers Univ., 1985), 39–40; Richard E. Slitor, "Rationale of the Present Tax Benefits for Homeowners," in Mitchell, *Federal Housing,* 10: 172.

10. Cohn, *Palace or Poorhouse,* ch. 6.

11. Robert Moore Fisher, *20 Years of Public Housing* (New York: Harper and Brothers Publishers, 1959), 24–27, 73–79; Sternlieb and Listokin, "Review of National Housing Policy," 15–16, 19.

12. Fisher, *20 Years,* 79–91; Nathaniel S. Keith, *Politics and the Housing Crisis Since 1930* (New York: Universe Books, 1973), 21–22, 27–29.

13. Gilbert Y. Steiner, *The State of Welfare* (Washington, DC: The Brookings Institution, 1971), 138–143.

14. Leonard Freedman, *Public Housing* (New York: Holt, Rinehart and Winston, Inc., 1969). Keith, *Politics and the Housing Crisis,* chs. 4–8, paints essentially the same picture.

15. Freedman, *Public Housing,* 173, quoting Charles T. Stewart, an official of NAREB, from "Public Housing—Wrong Way Program," *U.S.A.—The Magazine of American Affairs* (June 1952): 91–98.

16. Freedman, *Public Housing,* 179–181.

17. The Bankhead-Jones Farm Tenant Act of 1937 was the earliest of these; see section 6, "A Legacy of Political Language" in ch. 2.

18. On the Indian Mutual Help Ownership Opportunity Program, which provides 61 percent of HUD assistance to Native American areas, see Stuart M. Butler, "Public Housing: From Tenants to Homeowners," from the *Heritage Foundation Backgrounder* (12 June 1984) delivered as testimony before the Joint Economic Committee and reprinted in *Congressional Record,* 98th Cong., 2nd sess., 27 Sept. 1984, 27502.

19. In most cases the poorest applicants for subsistence homesteading had been weeded out to insure the experiments against avoidable risks. Ghirardo, *Building New Communities,* 168–174.

20. John C. Weicher, *Housing* (Washington, DC: American Enterprise Institute for Public Policy Research, 1980), 43.

21. "Text of President Kennedy's March 9 Housing Message," *Congressional Quarterly Weekly Report,* 10 March 1961, 402.

22. U.S. Commission on Civil Rights, *Homeownership for Lower-Income Families* (Washington, DC: U.S. Government Printing Office, 1971), 4–5 n 35, 36; Freedman, *Public Housing,* 188.

23. *Congressional Record,* 90th Cong., 1st sess., 20 April 1967, 10364–10365, 10403–10404.

24. "Percy explains home ownership plan," *Christian Science Monitor,* 19 April 1967, 12.

25. *Congressional Record*, 90th Cong., 1st sess., 20 April 1967, 10289.

26. Senator Percy, Ibid., 10300.

27. Senator Thurmond, Ibid., 10289.

28. Senator Baker, Ibid., 10292.

29. Senator Byrd, Ibid., 10294.

30. Senator Brooke, Ibid., 10293.

31. *The New Republic*, 14 Oct. 1967, 7; Freedman, *Public Housing*, 188–189; Keith, *Politics and the Housing Crisis*, 182–183. Keith alleges partisan motives on behalf of the Percy bill's Republican sponsors, and that many of them would have voted against the bill if it had ever come to the floor.

32. "The Crisis of the Cities—The President's Message to the Congress on Urban Progress," *Weekly Compilation of Presidential Documents*, 26 Feb. 1968, 330.

33. U.S. Commission on Civil Rights, *Homeownership*, 8.

34. U.S. Commission on Civil Rights, *Homeownership*, 82–84, 64–65. The focus of the study was on the perpetuation of segregation under Sec. 235; white participants were being sold new homes in the suburbs while minority participants were steered to used homes in ghettoes or in neighborhoods of changing racial composition.

35. Rachel G. Bratt, *Rebuilding a Low-Income Housing Policy* (Philadelphia: Temple Univ. Press, 1989), 93, 135–144.

36. "Homeownership Subsidy," *CQ Weekly Report*, 25 Oct. 1975, 2259.

37. "Housing Notes," *CQ Weekly Report*, 20 Sept. 1975, 1998.

38. *CQ Weekly Report*, 25 Oct. 1975, 2259.

39. Weicher, *Housing*, 50–51, 122–123.

40. Keith, *Politics and the Housing Crisis*, 131.

41. Freedman, *Public Housing*, 187–188; on Weaver's reservations Freedman cites the Senate *Hearings, Housing Legislation of 1967*, Pt. 1, 72–75.

42. *Congressional Record*, 89th Cong., 1st sess., 18 Feb. 1965, 3065.

43. Freedman, *Public Housing*, 188.

44. Mittie Olion Chandler, *Urban Homesteading* (New York, NY, and Westport, CT: Greenwood Press, 1988), 38. The quote is Chandler's characterization of the critics' view; she disagrees with them.

45. Howard J. Sumka, "Creative Reuse of the Existing Stock," in *Housing America's Poor*, ed. Salins, 6: 118–122, 127–134.

46. David C. Schwartz, Richard C. Ferlauto and Daniel N. Hoffman, *A New Public Housing Policy for America* (Philadelphia: Temple Univ. Press, 1988), 240–241.

47. Eventually President Reagan appropriated the symbols of agrarian republicanism for the entire privatization effort: "Privatization follows in the great tradition of free enterprise and private ownership of property that has long been a part of American history, from the initial sale of government lands under the Northwest Ordinance to the homestead program that brought the pioneers to the American West over 100 years ago . . . ,"

Public Papers of the Presidents of the United States: Ronald Reagan, 1987, bk. II (Washington, DC: U.S. Government Printing Office, 1989), 992.

48. Peter Dreier, "Public Housing for Sale: Private Project," *New Republic,* 4 Aug. 1986, 13; Mitchell, *Federal Housing Policy,* 203.

49. Testimony before the JECs Sub-committee on Monetary and Fiscal Policy (27 Sept. 1984), as published in *Congressional Record,* 98th Cong., 2nd sess., 27 Sept. 1984, 27499.

50. *Congressional Record,* 98th Cong., 2nd sess., 26 Sept. 1984, 27375.

51. Michael A. Stegman, "The Role of Public Housing in a Revitalized National Housing Policy," in *Building Foundations,* ed. Denise DiPasquale and Langley C. Keyes (Philadelphia: Univ. of Pennsylvania Press, 1990), 13: 357–358; Schwartz, Ferlauto and Hoffman, *New Public Housing Policy,* 54.

52. *Congressional Quarterly Almanac:* 98th Cong., 1st sess., 1983, vol. 39 (Washington, DC: Congressional Quarterly, Inc., 1984), 277.

53. Representative Kemp, *Congressional Record,* 99th Cong., 2nd sess., 11 June 1986, 13221.

54. Representative Courter, Ibid., 13222.

55. Ibid., 13234–13246. The Democrats from the housing subcommittee were apparently caught by surprise, later claiming they had been "sandbagged" by Kemp; see David Rapp, "House Ignores Veto Threats, Passes $16 Billion Housing Bill," *CQ Weekly Report,* 13 June 1987, 1238.

56. *Congressional Record,* 100th Cong., 1st sess., 10 June 1987, 15239–15241, 15265.

57. Most of this paragraph is based on *Congressional Record,* 100th Cong., 1st sess., 10 June 1987, 15344–15352.

58. *Congressional Record,* 102nd Cong., 1st sess., 6 June 1991, H4106.

59. Stegman, "Role of Public Housing," 358–359.

60. "Senate Offers Its Hand to Cabinet Nominees," *CQ Weekly Report,* 28 Jan. 1989, 151–154.

61. House subcommittee on Veterans Affairs, Housing and Urban Development, and Independent Agencies, *Hearings on Departments of VA, HUD, and Independent Agencies Appropriations for 1990,* pt. 7, 19 April 1989, 33.

62. Robert Kuttner, "Bleeding Heart Conservative," *New Republic,* 11 June 1990, 22.

63. Phil Kuntz, "Kemp, Key Democrats on Hill Joust Over HUD Programs," *CQ Weekly Report,* 14 Oct. 1989, 2721–2722; Kuntz, "In Turnabout, House Banking Advances HUD Reform Bill," *CQ Weekly Report,* 11 Nov. 1989, 3067–3069.

64. Phil Kuntz, "HUD Reform Package Clears On Edge of Adjournment," *CQ Weekly Report,* 25 Nov. 1989, 3242–3243.

65. Jill Zuckman, "Kemp Outlines HOPE Proposal To Skeptical House Panel," *CQ Weekly Report,* 17 March 1990, 839.

66. Paula Dwyer with Peter Hong, "How Kemp Built a Housing Bill That May Stand Up in Congress," *Business Week,* 2 July 1990, 43; Jill Zuckman, "HUD's Kemp Comes Out on Top In Negotiations With Senate," *CQ Weekly Report,* 30 June 1990, 2059–2060.

67. Fred Barnes, "White House Watch: Prince of Poverty," *New Republic*, 8 Oct. 1990, 10–12.

68. Kuttner, "Bleeding Heart Conservative," 23–24.

69. "Remarks on Signing the Cranston-Gonzalez National Affordable Housing Act," *Public Papers of the Presidents of the United States: George Bush 1990*, bk. I (Washington, DC: U.S. Government Printing Office, 1991), 1698.

70. Jason DeParle, "Amid Housing Crisis, a Bitter Feud Between Baronies Over U.S. Policy," *New York Times*, 23 Oct. 1991, sec. A6.

71. "Panel Protects Domestic Funds By Killing Space Station," *CQ Weekly Report*, 18 May 1991, 1289; Alissa J. Rubin and Jill Zuckman, "House Revives Space Station With Cuts to Housing," *CQ Weekly Report*, 8 June 1991, 1494.

72. *Congressional Record*, 102nd Cong., 1st sess., 6 June 1991, H4105.

73. Jill Zuckman, "Milkulski Trims Carefully To Pay Cost of Freedom," *CQ Weekly Report*, 13 July 1991, 1890.

74. Alissa J. Rubin, "VA-HUD Money Rearranged For Favored Programs," *CQ Weekly Report*, 28 Sept. 1991, 2778; DeParle, "Amid Housing Crisis"; Jill Zuckman and Rubin, "Social Program Lobbyists Dig In As NASA Looks To Senate," *CQ Weekly Report*, 15 June 1991, 1579.

75. Jason DeParle, "Government Housing Plan Aims to End Tenants' Dependence on Public Aid," *New York Times*, 20 Feb. 1992, sec. A13.

76. Jeffrey L. Katz, "Room for Improvement: Can Cisneros Fix HUD?" *CQ Weekly Report*, 10 April 1993, 914, 919; Katz, "Special Report: Income Security," Ibid., 896; George Hager, "Panel Approves Supplemental With No Money for Jobs Plan," *CQ Weekly Report*, 15 May 1993, 1214–1215; Hager, "Supplemental Spending Bills Get Green Light in House," *CQ Weekly Report*, 29 May 1993, 1346–1347; *CQ Weekly Report*, 23 Oct. 1993, 2887; *CQ Weekly Report*, 23 April 1994, 2575; *CQ Weekly Report*, 11 May 1996, 1334; Steven A. Holmes, "Kemp's Legacy as Housing Secretary One of Ideas, Not Accomplishments," *New York Times*, 20 Aug. 1996, sec. A15.

77. Representative Clay, *Congressional Record*, 102nd Cong., 1st sess., 6 June 1991, H4108.

78. Representative Waters, Ibid., H4109.

79. Representative Stokes, Ibid., H4110.

NOTES TO CHAPTER 4:
WELFARE AND WORK

1. Josephine Chapin Brown, *Public Relief 1929–1939* (New York: Henry Holt and Co., 1940), 10.

2. Michael B. Katz, *In the Shadow of the Poorhouse* (New York: Basic Books, Inc., Publishers, 1986), 25–35, 91–94.

3. Walter I. Trattner, *From Poor Law to Welfare State*, 3rd ed. (New York: The Free Press, 1984), 89–90; Brown, *Public Relief*, 39–40.

4. Katz, *Shadow of the Poorhouse*, 52–57; Brown, *Public Relief*, 16–17.

5. Trattner, *From Poor Law*, 92–99; June Axinn and Herman Levin, *Social Welfare*, 3rd ed. (New York: Longman, 1992), 94–97, 107; Katz, *Shadow of the Poorhouse*, 66–80.

6. Katz, *Shadow of the Poorhouse*, 80–84, 147–148.

7. James Leiby, *A History of Social Welfare and Social Work in the United States* (New York: Columbia Univ. Press, 1978), 176–179; Roy Lubove, *The Struggle for Social Security 1900–1935*, 2nd ed. (Pittsburgh: Univ. of Pittsburgh Press, 1986), 94–96; Katz, *Shadow of the Poorhouse*, 154–156.

8. Katz, *Shadow of the Poorhouse*, 148; Lubove, *Struggle for Social Security*, 145.

9. Brown, *Public Relief*, 21–26.

10. Katz, *Shadow of the Poorhouse*, 182–186.

11. Theda Skocpol, *Protecting Soldiers and Mothers* (Cambridge, MA: The Belknap Press, 1992), 267–278; Lubove, *Struggle for Social Security*, 114–119.

12. Lubove, *Struggle for Social Security*, chs. 1–2, 4, 7.

13. Skocpol, *Soldiers and Mothers*, 424–471; Lubove, *Struggle for Social Security*, 96–109; Katz, *Shadow of the Poorhouse*, 118–129; Joel F. Handler and Yeheskel Hasenfeld, *The Moral Construction of Poverty* (Newbury Park, CA: Sage Publications, 1991), 63–74; Trattner, *From Poor Law*, 112–114, 120, 209–211.

14. Skocpol, *Soldiers and Mothers*, 471–479; Lubove, *Struggle for Social Security*, 109–111, 135–143; Handler and Hasenfeld, *Moral Construction*, 75–76; Brown, *Public Relief*, 26–31; Axinn and Levin, *Social Welfare*, 141.

15. Brown, *Public Relief*, 9–10, 13–16.

16. Axinn and Levin, *Social Welfare*, 147–149; Trattner, *From Poor Law*, ch. 12.

17. William R. Brock, *Welfare, Democracy, and the New Deal* (Cambridge and New York: Cambridge Univ. Press, 1988), 84–102, 124–139; Brown, *Public Relief*, 63–128; Trattner, *From Poor Law*, 257–264; Katz, *Shadow of the Poorhouse*, 213–217.

18. "Annual Message to Congress on the State of the Union" (8 Dec. 1931), in *Public Papers of the Presidents of the United States: Herbert Hoover 1931* (Washington, DC: U.S. Government Printing Office, 1976), 593.

19. Brown, *Public Relief*, 112; Lubove, *Struggle for Social Security*, 166–168; Handler and Hasenfeld, *Moral Construction*, 91.

20. Brown, *Public Relief*, 146–154; Axinn and Levin, *Social Welfare*, 185–187.

21. "Annual Message to the Congress" (4 Jan. 1935), in *The Public Papers and Addresses of Franklin D. Roosevelt*, ed. Samuel I. Rosenman, vol. 4 (New York: Random House, 1938), 19–20.

22. Brock, *Welfare, Democracy, and the New Deal*, 256–265, 270–271, 332–333; James T. Patterson, *America's Struggle Against Poverty 1900–1985*, 2nd ed. (Cambridge, MA: Harvard Univ. Press, 1986), 59.

23. Axinn and Levin, *Social Welfare*, 187–198; Trattner, *From Poor Law*, 270–274; Brown, *Public Relief*, 163–169; Katz, *Shadow of the Poorhouse*, 235–239; Edwin E. Witte, *The Development of the Social Security Act* (Madison, WI: Univ. of Wisconsin Press, 1962).

24. Brock, *Welfare, Democracy, and the New Deal*, 351–353.

25. Stephen Kemp Bailey, *Congress Makes a Law* (New York: Columbia Univ. Press, 1950), 8–28, 41–60.

26. Senator Murray, *The Congressional Record*, 79th Cong., 1st sess., 22 Jan. 1945, 378.

27. Senator Tobey, *Congressional Record*, 79th Cong., 1st sess., 25 Sept. 1945, 8960.

28. For typical examples, see *Congressional Record*, 79th Cong., 1st sess., 25 Sept. 1945, 8958–8962, and, 28 Sept. 1945, 9047–9062. A summary of the leading conservative arguments can be found in Bailey, *Congress Makes a Law*, 130–131.

29. Bailey, *Congress Makes a Law*, ch. 11.

30. James L. Sundquist, *Politics and Policy* (Washington, DC: The Brookings Institution, 1968), chs. 2–3.

31. Patterson, *America's Struggle*, 92–94; Martha Derthick, *Policymaking for Social Security* (Washington, DC: The Brookings Institution, 1979), 21–27, 213–227, 273–274; Brown, *Public Relief*, 368–374; Gilbert Y. Steiner, *Social Insecurity* (Chicago: Rand McNally and Co., 1966), 50–59.

32. David Brian Robertson and Dennis R. Judd, *The Development of American Public Policy* (Glenview, IL: Scott, Foresman and Co., 1989), 218–220; Patterson, *America's Struggle*, 101–103.

33. Trattner, *From Poor Law*, 292–293.

34. Patterson, *America's Struggle*, 89–90, 106–110.

35. Ibid., 67–69, 87–88; Axinn and Levin, *Social Welfare*, 237–238.

36. Patterson, *America's Struggle*, 90–91.

37. Ibid., 129–132; Sundquist, *Politics and Policy*, 125–130; Axinn and Levin, *Social Welfare*, 240–245; Steiner, *Social Insecurity*, 37–47, 172–175.

38. "Statement by the President Upon Approving the Public Welfare Amendments Bill" (26 July 1962), in *Public Papers of the Presidents: John F. Kennedy 1962* (Washington, DC: U.S. Government Printing Office, 1963), 580. See also "Annual Message to the Congress on the State of the Union" (11 Jan. 1962), Ibid., 8. In this earlier statement he used a phrase identical to the first sentence quoted here, with the telling difference that he said "services *instead* of support" (emphasis added).

39. "Special Message to the Congress on Public Welfare Programs" (1 Feb. 1962), Ibid., 103.

40. Representative Herlong, *Congressional Record*, 87th Cong., 2nd sess., 15 March 1962, 4276. For similar examples by other representatives, see Ibid., 4261, 4268.

41. Patterson, *America's Struggle*, 126–129, 133–135; Sundquist, *Politics and Policy*, 112–125, 131–137; Sar A. Levitan, *The Great Society's Poor Law* (Baltimore: The Johns Hopkins Press, 1969), 13–18.

42. Sundquist, *Politics and Policy*, 137–145; Patterson, *America's Struggle*, 135–141; Levitan, *Great Society's Poor Law*, 18–37.

43. John C. Donovan, *The Politics of Poverty*, 2nd ed. (Indianapolis and New York: Pegasus, 1973), 18.

44. "Remarks at a Reception for Members of the American Society of Newspaper Editors" (17 April 1964), in *Public Papers of the Presidents: Lyndon B. Johnson 1963–1964* (Washington, DC: U.S. Government Printing Office, 1965), 1:414.

45. "Remarks Upon Signing the Economic Opportunity Act" (20 Aug. 1964), Ibid., vol. 2, 989. One anecdote has it that Johnson so disliked the word "welfare" that he habitually referred to HEW as his "Department of Health and Education;" Daniel Patrick Moynihan, *The Politics of a Guaranteed Income* (New York: Random House, 1973), 130; Vincent J. Burke and Vee Burke, *Nixon's Good Deed* (New York: Columbia Univ. Press, 1974), 44. Perhaps LBJ was prophetic: HEW became the Department of Health and Human Services under President Carter.

46. *Congressional Record*, 88th Cong., 2nd sess., 8 Aug. 1964, 18651.

47. Senator Yarborough, *Congressional Record*, 88th Cong., 2nd sess., 22 July 1964, 16632.

48. Sunquist, *Politics and Policy*, 145–151; Levitan, *Great Society's Poor Law*, 37–47; Donovan, *Politics of Poverty*, 33–34.

49. Patterson, *America's Struggle*, 142–148; Donovan, *Politics of Poverty*, chs. 5, 8; Daniel Patrick Moynihan, *Maximum Feasible Misunderstanding* (New York: Free Press, 1969). Spending on the EOA programs was always but a fraction of federal spending on public assistance programs such as AFDC and Old Age Assistance; Robertson and Judd, *Development of American Public Policy*, 223.

50. Margaret Weir, *Politics and Jobs* (Princeton, NJ: Princeton Univ. Press, 1992), 83–89.

51. Patterson, *America's Struggle*, 179–183. Grassroots welfare lobbying receded with the death of the leader of the National Welfare Rights Organization in 1973 and the increasingly conservative political climate.

52. Ibid., 172–173.

53. Gilbert Y. Steiner, *The State of Welfare* (Washington, DC: The Brookings Institution, 1971), 43–50.

54. *Congressional Record*, 90th Cong., 1st sess., 17 Aug. 1967, 23052, 23058.

55. *Congressional Quarterly Weekly Report*, 22 Dec. 1967, 2597–2601.

56. *Congressional Record*, 90th Cong., 1st sess., 15 Nov. 1967, 32592.

57. *CQ Weekly Report*, 22 Dec. 1967, 2600; Burke and Burke, *Nixon's Good Deed*, 35–36; Axinn and Levin, *Social Welfare*, 250–252; Trattner, *From Poor Law*, 305–307.

58. I. Garfinkel and Sarah McLanahan, *Single Mothers and Their Children* (Washington, DC: Urban Institute Press, 1986), 118–136.

59. Burke and Burke, *Nixon's Good Deed*, 12–26, 36–39; Daniel Patrick Moynihan, *The Politics of a Guaranteed Income* (New York: Random House, 1973), 49–51, 55–58, 124–134; Patterson, *America's Struggle*, 185–192.

60. Moynihan, *Guaranteed Income*, 245, 10–11.

61. Ibid., 61–62.

62. Ibid., 182–183; Burke and Burke, *Nixon's Good Deed*, 110.

63. Moynihan, *Guaranteed Income*, 67–74; Burke and Burke, *Nixon's Good Deed*, 41–43; Steiner, *State of Welfare*, 110–116; Kenneth M. Bowler, *The Nixon Guaranteed Income Proposal* (Cambridge, MA: Ballinger Publishing Co., 1974), 39–42.

64. "Remarks at a Luncheon of the National Alliance of Businessmen" (15 March 1969), in *Public Papers of the Presidents: Richard Nixon 1969* (Washington, DC: U.S. Government Printing Office, 1971), 221.

65. Bowler, *Nixon Guaranteed Income*, 42–52; Moynihan, *Guaranteed Income*, 79–81, 96–99, 135–137, 143–148, 160–166, 170–184; Burke and Burke, *Nixon's Good Deed*, 43–82.

66. "Special Message to the Congress on Forthcoming Legislative Proposals Concerning Domestic Programs" (14 April 1969), in *Public Papers of the Presidents: Richard Nixon 1969*, 286.

67. Bowler, *Nixon's Guaranteed Income*, 52–69; Moynihan, *Guaranteed Income*, 184–204, 213–216; Burke and Burke, *Nixon's Good Deed*, 83–107.

68. Moynihan, *Guaranteed Income*, 218–220.

69. "Address to the Nation on Domestic Programs" (8 Aug. 1969), in *Public Papers of the Presidents: Richard Nixon 1969*, 639–641, 644–645.

70. Burke and Burke, *Nixon's Good Deed*, 111.

71. Moynihan, *Guaranteed Income*, 250–396; Burke and Burke, *Nixon's Good Deed*, 125–150.

72. Moynihan, *Guaranteed Income*, 398–428

73. Ibid., 426.

74. Ibid., 428–438; Burke and Burke, *Nixon's Good Deed*, 132–135, 152.

75. Representative Foreman, *Congressional Record*, 91st Cong., 2nd sess., 16 April 1970, 12028.

76. Representative Ashbrook, *Congressional Record*, 91st Cong., 2nd sess., 15 April 1970, 11877.

77. Moynihan, *Guaranteed Income*, 439–538; Burke and Burke, *Nixon's Good Deed*, 152–165; Bowler, *Nixon's Guaranteed Income*, 72.

78. Bowler, *Nixon's Guaranteed Income*, 83–134, 148–149; Burke and Burke, *Nixon's Good Deed*, 164–180; Trattner, *From Poor Law*, 321–322.

79. "Statement on Signing a Bill Amending the Social Security Act" (28 Dec. 1971), in *Public Papers of the Presidents: Richard Nixon 1969*, 1212–1213.

80. Bowler, *Nixon's Guaranteed Income*, 135–159; Burke and Burke, *Nixon's Good Deed*, 180–187; "Senate Rejects Ribicoff, Nixon Welfare Reform Plans," *CQ Weekly Report*, 7 Oct. 1972, 2628–2629.

81. "Welfare Reform-Remarks at a News Briefing on Goals and Guidelines" (2 May 1977), in *Public Papers of the Presidents: Jimmy Carter 1977*, bk. I (Washington, DC: U.S. Government Printing Office, 1977), 771.

82. Laurence E. Lynn, Jr., and David deF. Whitman, *The President as Policymaker* (Philadelphia: Temple Univ. Press, 1981), 37–51, 67–238; Handler and Hasenfeld, *Moral Construction*, 160–164.

83. Lynn and Whitman, *President as Policymaker*, 238–249. On the CETA program, see Weir, *Politics and Jobs*, 123–129.

84. Representative Walker, *Congressional Record*, 96th Cong., 1st sess., 7 Nov. 1979, 31337.

85. Lynn and Whitman, *President as Policymaker*, 249–255.

86. Harrison Donnelly and Elizabeth Wehr, "Candidates Differ on Federal Role in Setting Social Policies," *CQ Weekly Report*, 25 Oct. 1980, 3197–3198; Robertson and Judd, *Development of American Public Policy*, 231.

87. *CQ Weekly Report*, 19 July 1980, 2032.

88. H. Donnelly, "Working Mothers' Benefits Cut in New AFDC Provisions in Reconciliation Measure," *CQ Weekly Report*, 15 Aug. 1981, 1493; Handler and Hasenfeld, *Moral Construction*, 170–175; Robertson and Judd, *Development of American Public Policy*, 231–233.

89. From *CQ Weekly Report*: H. Donnelly, "More Cuts Proposed in Social Programs," 13 Feb. 1982, 240–241; Andy Plattner, "Congress in 1982: Stirrings of Independence," 31 Dec. 1982, 3157; Laura B. Weiss and E. Wehr, "New Cuts in Social Programs Proposed," 5 Feb. 1983, 309; Dale Tate, "House Approves $936 Billion Budget for '84," 26 March 1983, 602–603; E. Wehr, Janet Hook and Pamela Fessler, "Entitlements Drive HHS Spending Up Again," 4 Feb. 1984, 183; P. Fessler, "Tax Hike Conferees Press On; Difficult Issues Still Pending," 16 June 1984, 1416; Jacqueline Calmes, "Conferees Begin to Reconcile Versions of Deficit-Cutting Bills," 7 Dec. 1985, 2551; J. Hook, "Deep New Cuts in Social Spending Proposed," 8 Feb. 1986, 222–223.

90. Patterson, *America's Struggle*, 215–219; Katz, *Shadow of the Poorhouse*, 276–277.

91. George Gilder, *Wealth and Poverty* (New York: Bantam, 1981).

92. Charles Murray, *Losing Ground* (New York: Basic Books, 1984).

93. "Address Before a Joint Session of Congress on the State of the Union" (4 Feb. 1986), in *Public Papers of the Presidents: Ronald Reagan 1986*, bk. I (Washington, DC: U.S. Government Printing Office, 1989), 128; see also "Message to the Congress on America's Agenda for the Future" (6 Feb. 1986), Ibid., 154.

94. These included the National Governors' Association, the American Public Welfare Association, two task forces under individual governors, and the American Enterprise Institute. See: The Working Seminar on Family and American Welfare Policy, *The New Consensus on Family and Welfare* (Washington, DC: American Enterprise Institute for Public Policy Research, 1987), 74–82; Robert D. Reischauer, "The Welfare Reform Legislation: Directions for the Future," in *Welfare Policy for the 1990s*, ed. P. Cottingham and D. Ellwood (Cambridge: Harvard Univ. Press, 1989), 1:10.

95. Mary Jo Bane and David Ellwood, "Slipping into and out of Poverty: The Dynamics of Spells," *Journal of Human Resources* 21, no. 1 (1986): 1–23.

96. A description and justification of the "new consensus" may be found in Lawrence M. Mead, *Beyond Entitlement* (New York: The Free Press, 1986). One of my largest disagreements with Mead's interpretation involves his characterization of the philosophical grounds of the consensus as something new. Although his name for it, "civic conservatism," is suggestive, he does not connect it with the republican tradition.

97. From *CQ Weekly Report:* Julie Rovner, "Welfare Reform: The Next Domestic Priority?" 27 Sept. 1986, 2281–2286; Stephen Gettinger, "Negotiators Adopt $12 Billion Deficit-Reduction Measure," 18 Oct. 1986, 2588; J. Rovner, "Congress Votes $114.78 Billion for Labor-HHS," 1 Nov. 1986, 2738.

98. From *CQ Weekly Report:* J. Rovner, "Congress Takes Ball and Runs After State of the Union Punt," 31 Jan. 1987, 206–208; J. Rovner, "Governors Jump-Start Welfare Reform Drive," 28 Feb. 1987, 376–378; J. Rovner, "House Democrats Unveil Welfare Blueprint . . . Senate Also Has Overhaul on Fast Track," 27 March 1987, 504–505.

99. J. Rovner, "Reagan Team Tears Into Democrats' Welfare Plan," *CQ Weekly Report,* 4 April 1987, 627; "Remarks at the Annual Meeting of the National Alliance of Business" (14 Sept. 1987), in *Public Papers of the Presidents: Ronald Reagan 1987,* bk. II (Washington, DC: U.S. Government Printing Office, 1989), 1032.

100. From *CQ Weekly Report:* Mark Willen, "Modified Welfare Reform Bill OK'd by House Subcommittee," 11 April 1987, 682–683; J. Rovner, "Reagan Endorses Revised GOP Welfare Plan," 8 Aug. 1987, 1811; Patrick L. Knudsen, "After Long, Bruising Battle, House Approves Welfare Bill," 19 Dec. 1987, 3157–3159.

101. From *CQ Weekly Report:* J. Rovner, "Governors Press Reagan, Bentsen on Welfare," 27 Feb. 1988, 512–513; J. Rovner, "Senate Finance Endorses Modified Welfare Bill," 23 April 1988, 1068–1070; J. Rovner, "Deep Schisms Still Imperial Welfare Overhaul," 18 June 1988, 1647–1650.

102. Senator Dole, *Congressional Record,* 100th Cong., 2nd sess., 16 June 1988, 14910.

103. J. Rovner, "Congress Clears Overhaul of Welfare System" and "Highlights, Welfare Overhaul Legislation," *CQ Weekly Report,* 1 Oct. 1988, 26699–26701.

104. Senator Moynihan, *Congressional Record,* 100th Cong., 2nd sess., 29 Sept. 1988, 26578.

105. Senator Armstrong, Ibid., 26581–26583.

106. Senator Biden, Ibid., 26593.

107. *Congressional Record,* 100th Cong., 1st sess., 16 Dec. 1987, 35825.

108. Jeffrey L. Katz, "If It All Sounds Familiar . . . ," *CQ Weekly Report,* 27 Feb. 1993, 459.

109. Gwen Ifill, "Clinton Proposes Welfare Overhaul Emphasizing Work," *New York Times,* 10 Sept. 1992, A1. The idea of a time limit with transitional assistance was taken from Harvard professor David Ellwood's book, *Poor Support* (N.Y.: Basic Books, Inc., 1988). Ellwood later cochaired the Clinton administration's task force on welfare reform.

110. Jason DeParle, "Clinton Idea Used to Limit Welfare," *New York Times*, 2 June 1993, A7; DeParle, "Clinton Aides See Problem with Vow to Limit Welfare," *New York Times*, 21 June 1993, A1; Jeffrey L. Katz, "GOP's Two-Year Welfare Limit Sends Message to Clinton," *CQ Weekly Report*, 13 Nov. 1993, 3131.

111. From *New York Times:* Jason DeParle, "Clinton Welfare Planners Outline Big Goals Financed by Big Savings," 3 Dec. 1993, A1; DeParle, "Change in Welfare is Likely to Need Big Jobs Program," 30 Jan. 1994, A1; DeParle, "Democrats Face Hard Choices in Welfare Overhaul," 22 Feb. 1994, A16; DeParle, "Eager Democrats Pre-empt Clinton on Welfare Change," 11 May 1994. From *CQ Weekly Report:* Jeffrey L. Katz, "Highlights of Clinton Plan," 22 Jan. 1994, 120; Katz, "Welfare Overhaul Forces Ready To Start Without Clinton," 2 April 1994, 800–3. Robert B. Reich, *Locked in the Cabinet* (N.Y.: Alfred A. Knopf, 1997), 178.

112. Jeffrey L. Katz, "Long-Awaited Welfare Proposal Would Make Gradual Changes," *CQ Weekly Report*, 18 June 1994, 1622–24.

113. "Message to the Congress Transmitting Proposed Welfare Reform Legislation" (21 June 1994), *Public Papers of the Presidents: William J Clinton 1994*, bk. I (Washington, DC: U.S. Government Printing Office, 1995), 1112. Later that year Clinton made the obligatory reference to FDR's quotation about relief being a narcotic; "Remarks to the Governor's Leadership Conference in New York City" (19 Oct. 1994), Ibid., bk. 11, 1801.

114. From *CQ Weekly Report:* Jeffrey L. Katz, "Chances for Overhaul in Doubt As Time for Action Dwindles," 30 July 1994, 2150; "Republicans' Initial Promise: 100-Day Debate on 'Contract,'" 12 Nov. 1994, 3217; Katz, "Broad Plan Alters Nature of Welfare Debate" and "Highlights of Welfare Proposal," 19 Nov. 1994, 3334–3336; Katz, "Parts of Welfare Plan Concern GOP Moderates, Governors," 10 Dec. 1994, 3510–3512. From *New York Times:* Jason DeParle, "New Majority's Agenda: Substantial Changes May Be Ahead" (section on Welfare), 11 Nov. 1994, A10; Robert Pear, "House G.O.P. Would Replace Scores of Programs for the Poor," 9 Dec. 1994; A1. Elizabeth Drew, *Showdown: The Struggle Between the Gingrich Congress and the Clinton White House* (N.Y.: Simon and Schuster, 1996), 81–85.

115. From *CQ Weekly Report:* Jeffrey L. Katz, "Key Members Seek To Expand State Role in Welfare Plan," 14 Jan. 1995, 159–162; Jeffrey L. Katz, with Alissa J. Rubin and Peter MacPherson, "Major Aspects of Welfare Bill Approved by Subcommittee," 18 Feb. 1995, 525–529; Katz and Rubin, "House Panel Poised to Approve GOP Welfare Overhaul Bill," 4 March 1995, 689–692. From *New York Times:* Robert Pear, "Republicans' Philosophical Discord Stalls Plan for Changes," 12 Jan. 1995, A10; Pear, "Democrats Call Republicans Too Lenient on Welfare," 11 Feb. 1995, 6; Pear, "House Backs Bill Undoing Decades of Welfare Policy," 25 March 1995, A1. Drew, *Showdown*, 88–92, 140–149.

116. Representative Menendez, *Congressional Record*, 104th Cong., 1st sess., 24 March 1995, H3738.

117. Representative Riggs, Ibid., H3741.

118. Representative Mica, Ibid., H3766.

119. Representative Burton, Ibid., H3772.

120. From *CQ Weekly Report:* Jeffrey L. Katz, "Key GOP Senators Back Giving States Leeway on Welfare," 29 April 1995, 1187; Katz, "Governors Sidelined In Welfare

Debate," 20 May 1995, 1423–1424; Katz, "Senate's Plan Falls in Line, Shifts Welfare to States," 25 May 1995, 1503–1505; Katz, "GOP Rift Delays Action on Welfare," 17 June 1995, 1747; Katz, "Senate GOP Puts Overhaul on Hold To Muster Votes," 12 Aug. 1995, 2443–2445; Katz, "Uneasy Compromise Reached On Welfare Overhaul," 16 Sep. 1995, 2804–2808. From *New York Times:* Robert Pear, "Senate Finance Panel Approves A Vast Restructuring of Welfare," 27 May 1995, A1; Pear, "Republican Squabble Delays Senate Action on Welfare Bill," 16 June 1995, A1; Pear, "Dole Offers a Welfare Plan, But Conservatives Reject It," 5 August 1995, A1; Robin Toner, "Senators Gain In Move to Pass A Welfare Bill," 15 Sep. 1995, A1; Toner, "Senate Approves Welfare Plan That Would End Aid Guarantee," 20 Sep. 1995, A1. Drew, *Showdown,* 279–283, 315.

121. The FDR quote was also common in the House debate, as well as later in the debates over the conference committee report; e.g. *Congressional Record,* 104th Cong., 1st sess.: (22 March 1995), H3530; (23 March 1995) H3704, H3729; (24 March 1995) H3740; (7 Aug. 1995), S11736; (7 Sep. 1995) S12769; (21 Dec. 1995) H15525; (22 Dec. 1995) S19159, S19169.

122. From *CQ Weekly Report:* Jeffrey L. Katz, "Internal Squabbles Interfere With Welfare Overhaul," 18 Nov. 1995, 3541; Katz, "Clinton Vows To Veto Overhaul Measure," 23 Dec. 1995, 3889–3991. From *New York Times:* Robert Pear, "Republicans in Accord on Welfare Bill," 15 Nov. 1995, A14; Pear, "House Passes Measure to Overhaul Welfare," 22 Dec. 1995, C19; Pear, "Welfare Bill Cleared by Congress And Now Awaits Clinton's Veto," 23 Dec. 1995, A1.

123. From *CQ Weekly Report:* George Hager and Alissa J. Rubin, "Hopes Fade for Breakthrough in Short or Long Term," 10 Feb. 1996, 350–354; Jeffrey L. Katz, "GOP Prepares To Act On Governors' Plan," 17 Feb. 1996, 394–395; Katz, "Ignoring Veto Threat, GOP Links Welfare, Medicaid," 25 May 1996, 1465–1467; Katz, "GOP May Move To Split Medicaid, Welfare," 22 June 1996, 1761–1762; Katz, "GOP's New Welfare Strategy Has Democrats Reassessing," 13 July 1996, 1969–1970; Katz, "Conferees May Determine Fate of Overhaul Bill," 20 July 1996, 2048–2051; Katz, "Welfare Showdown Looms As GOP Readies Plan," 27 July 1995, 2115–2119. Robert Pear, "Senate Approves Sweeping Changes in Welfare Policy," *New York Times,* 24 July 1996, A1.

124. Senator Dorgan, *Congressional Record,* 104th Cong., 2nd sess., 18 July 1996, S8094.

125. Jeffrey L. Katz, "After 60 Years, Most Control Is Passing to States" and "Provisions of Welfare Bill," *CQ Weekly Report,* 3 Aug. 1996, 2190–2194. Robert Pear, "Clinton Says He'll Sign Bill Overhauling Welfare System," *New York Times,* 1 Aug. 1996, A1.

126. "Clinton Says Welfare Bill Is a 'Real Step Forward,' " *CQ Weekly Report,* 3 Aug. 1996, 2216.

127. See, for examples from the 1996 debates, *Congressional Record,* 104th Cong., 2nd sess.: (18 July 1996), H7803, H7980, S8092; (19 July 1996), S8337; (23 July 1996), S8495, S8509; (30 July 1996), H8670; (31 July 1996), H9396, H94112; (1 Aug. 1996), S9353, S9355, S9372, S9395.

128. Among poverty policy analysts, a popular approach to the "bad jobs" problem is that of "making work pay" through such measures as supplementing low wages (e.g., the Earned Income Tax Credit) and guaranteeing health insurance for all workers. I briefly address this concept in section 2 of the concluding chapter (ch. 6).

NOTES TO CHAPTER 5:
CAPITAL ASSETS AND THE POOR

1. That is, machinery, tools, equipment, vehicles, buildings, patents and other intellectual property, and so forth.

2. Louis O. Kelso and Mortimer J. Adler, *The Capitalist Manifesto* (New York: Random House, 1958). The first published statement of Kelso's ideas was an obscure article, "Karl Marx: The Almost Capitalist," in *The Bar Association Journal* (March 1957), which offered Kelso's critique of Marxist economics, but *The Capitalist Manifesto* is a much fuller, better-known and more easily accessible early exposition of his ideas.

3. Kelso and Adler, *Capitalist Manifesto,* 142–144.

4. Ibid., 229–231.

5. Ibid., 233–244; Louis O. Kelso and Mortimer J. Adler, *The New Capitalists* (New York: Random House, 1961).

6. Louis O. Kelso and Patricia Hetter Kelso, *Democracy and Economic Power* (Cambridge: Ballinger Publishing Co., 1986), 52–53; Stuart M. Speiser, *A Piece of the Action* (New York: Van Nostrand Reinhold Co., 1977), 163–168.

7. Kurland is still active in promoting Kelso's ideas as President of the Center for Economic and Social Justice in Washington, DC. <www.cesj.org>

8. Speiser, *Piece of the Action,* 143–162. The text of "The Full Production Act of 19—" is in the appendix to Louis O. Kelso and Patricia Hetter, *Two-Factor Theory* (New York: Vintage Books, 1967).

9. Subcommittee on Fiscal Policy of the Congressional Joint Economic Committee, 90th Cong., 2nd sess., *Hearings on Income Maintenance Programs,* v. II, 11–27 June 1968, 633–652.

10. Senate Finance Committee, 91st Cong., 1st sess., *Hearings on the Tax Reform Act of 1969,* pt. 2, 11–12 Sept. 1969, 1391–1505.

11. Ibid., 1404–1406 (emphasis in original.)

12. House Ways and Means Committee, 91st Cong., 1st sess., *Hearings on Social Security and Welfare Proposals,* pt. 4, 31 Oct. 1969, 1357–1402.

13. Ibid., 1359.

14. Speiser, *Piece of the Action,* 93–125. Speiser reprints Samuelson's statement in its entirety, subjecting it to a detailed and cogent analysis. For a more recent critique of Kelso's concept of "productiveness," see Alan Zundel, "Kelso's Binary Economy as Social Ethics," in the *Journal of Socio-Economics* (forthcoming in 2000).

15. Speiser, *Piece of the Action,* 163, 167–170, 191.

16. House Ways and Means Committee, 92nd Cong., 2nd sess., *Hearings on Tax Proposals Affecting Private Pension Plans,* pt. 3, 16 May 1972, 122–133, 647–720; Senate Commerce Committee Subcommittee on Surface Transportation, 93rd Cong., 1st. sess., *Hearings on Northeastern Railroad Transportation Crisis,* 28 Feb. 1973, 89–149; House Ways and Means Committee, 93rd Cong., 1st sess., *Hearings on General Tax Reform,* pt. 2, 9 March 1973, 793–828.

17. Senate Finance Committee Subcommittee on Financial Markets, 93rd Cong., 1st sess., *Hearings on the Impact of Institutional Investors in the Stock Market,* pt. 2, 24 Sep. 1973, 1–56.

18. Speiser, *Piece of the Action,* 191–195.

19. *The Congressional Record,* 93rd Cong., 1st sess,. 11 Dec. 1973, 40752–40753, 40756.

20. Senate Finance Committee, *Impact of Institutional Investors,* 55.

21. Speiser, *Piece of the Action,* 1–9, 188, 212. On Long's pushing of ESOPs, Speiser offers this quote (p. 203): "Just send us those tired, labor-plagued, competition-weary companies, and ESOP will breathe new life into them! ESOP is better than Geritol. It will revitalize capitalism. It will increase productivity. It will improve labor relations. It will promote economic justice. It will save our economic system. It will make our form of government and our concept of freedom prevail over those who don't agree with us!"

22. Tom Arrandale, "Capital Formation: New Tax Incentives Needed?" *Congressional Quarterly Weekly Report,* 9 Aug. 1975, 1757–1761; Daniel J. Balz, "Economic Report: Business presses changes in tax code to help investors," *National Journal,* 7, 30 Aug. 1975, 1229–1236. The incentives for saving included modifications of Individual Retirement Accounts (IRAs), which were created under the same 1974 pension reform act which first recognized ESOPs, and a proposal for Individual Savings Accounts with favorable tax treatment similar to IRAs but not limited to retirement uses. Ford's Broadened Stock Ownership Plan (BSOP) went nowhere, criticized in part because its tax deductions would mostly benefit better-off households.

23. Speiser, *Piece of the Action,* 207–209.

24. Congressional Joint Economic Committee (JEC), 94th Cong., 1st sess., *Hearings on Employee Stock Ownership Plans,* Parts 1–2, 11–12 Dec. 1975; Speiser, *Piece of the Action,* 230–239. The hearings record contains a document (pp. 928–949) that is very pertinent to this study: Larry Good, "Historical Perspectives on ESOP: The Homestead Debates." Good shows the correspondence between the arguments for and against homesteading and those for and against ESOPs. Both sets of arguments involve similar issues: revenue loss to the government (giving away the public lands, tax benefits for ESOPs), the potential for stimulating economic growth, the role of savings in accumulating wealth, concerns about benefiting the wrong people, and so forth.

25. JEC, 94th Cong., 2nd sess., *1976 Joint Economic Report,* 10 March 1976, 98–100; Speiser, *Piece of the Action,* 251–253.

26. JEC, *1976 Joint Economic Report,* 100.

27. The CFP relied upon savings and tax subsidies to create new capital owners, with a surtax on undistributed corporate profits to induce higher dividend payouts and more equity financing; John McClaughry, ed., *Expanded Ownership* (Fond du Lac, Wisconsin: Sabre Foundation, 1972).

28. JEC staff, 94th Cong., 2nd sess., *Broadening the Ownership of New Capital: ESOPs and Other Alternatives* (Washington, DC: U.S. Government Printing Office, 17 June 1976); Speiser, *Piece of the Action,* 253–258.

29. Brief descriptions of the nineteen ESOP laws passed from 1973 to 1986 may be found in Joseph Raphael Blasi, *Employee Ownership: Revolution or Ripoff?* (Cambridge: Ballinger Publishing Co., 1988), 33–38.

30. These appearances continued regularly throughout the 1970s and 1980s, the latest I am aware of being before the House Ways and Means Committee Subcommittee on Human Resources, 101st Cong., 1st sess., *Hearings on How To Help the Working Poor, and Problems of the Working Poor,* 21 March 1989, 177–223. Long retired in 1986, and Kelso died in 1991.

31. Michael Sherraden, "Rethinking Social Welfare: Towards Assets," *Social Policy* 18 (1988): 37–43; "Stakeholding: Notes on a Theory of Welfare Based on Assets," *Social Services Review* 64 (1990): 580–601; *Assets and the Poor* (Armonk, NY: M. E. Sharpe, Inc., 1991).

32. Michael Sherraden, interviewed by author by telephone, 7 May 1998.

33. Sherraden, *Assets and the Poor,* 191–192.

34. Sherraden telephone interview, 7 May 1998.

35. Cheryl Rene Rodriguez, *Women, Microenterprise, and the Politics of Self-Help* (New York: Garland Publishing, Inc., 1995), 51, 62–63, 86–93.

36. Sherraden telephone interview, 7 May 1998; Ray Boshara (former aide to Representative Hall and on the Select Committee on Hunger, currently with CFED), interviewed by author by telephone, 7 May 1998.

37. Boshara telephone interview, 7 May 1998; Sherraden telephone interview, 7 May 1998; see also ch. 5, section 3, "A Brief Moment in the Spotlight."

38. *Congressional Record,* 101st Cong., 2nd sess., 26 June 1990, H4207–4210.

39. Boshara telephone interview, 7 May 1998; Rodriguez, *Women, Microenterprise, and the Politics of Self-Help,* 81, 93–110; *Congressional Record,* 102nd Cong., 1st sess., 9 May 1991, E1667–1668, and 13 May 1991, E1720.

40. House Select Committee on Hunger, 102nd Cong., 1st sess., *Hearings on New Strategies For Alleviating Poverty: Building Hope By Building Assets,* 9 Oct. 1991, 3, 29, 82.

41. Ibid., 13.

42. *Congressional Record,* 102nd Cong., 1st sess., 16 Oct. 1991, H7975–7978.

43. Representative Ireland, Ibid., 2 Oct. 1991, H7298; Representative Pelosi, Ibid., 26 Nov. 1991, E4186.

44. Representative Hall, Ibid., 6 Nov. 1991, E3737.

45. Senator Bradley, Ibid., 26 Nov. 1991, S18403.

46. *Congressional Record,* 102nd Cong., 1st sess., 23 Oct. 1991, S15091. For the history of the recent welfare reform effort, see ch. 4, section 6, "The End of Welfare."

47. Sherraden telephone interview, 7 May 1998.

48. *Congressional Record,* 103rd Cong., 2nd sess., 21 June 1994, S7308–7312.

49. For example, see Ibid., 11 April 1994, S4077–4083; Welfare Innovation and Empowerment Act of 1995, 104th Cong., 1st sess., H.R. 781.

50. *Congressional Record,* 104th Cong., 2nd sess., 18 July 1996, S8149, S8296, S8368.

51. Public Law 104–193, Title I, Section 404(h).

52. Center for Social Development, George Warren Brown School of Social Work at Washington Univ., *CSD Update* 3 (Fall/Winter 1997/98):1; John Schmeltzer, "Savings Program for Poor Gets a Lift," *Chicago Tribune,* 24 Sep. 1997, sec. 3, 1.

53. Public Law 105–285, Title IV.

54. Edward N. Wolff, *Top Heavy: A Study of the Increasing Inequality of Wealth in America* (New York: The Twentieth Century Fund Press, 1995).

55. This is not the only problem with his FCP; some have also expressed the worry that such a large scale use of credit would be inflationary. Kelso's ideas are discussed further in the concluding chapter.

NOTES TO CHAPTER 6:
CONCLUSION: INDEPENDENCE
IN A POSTINDUSTRIAL ECONOMY

1. The evaluation work by Michael Sherraden and his associates will address this issue to some extent. For some early assessments, see: Gautam N. Yamada and Michael Sherraden, "Effects of Assets on Attitudes and Behaviors: Advance Test of a Social Policy Proposal," *Social Work Research* 40 (March 1997): 3–11; and Deborah Page-Adams and Michael Sherraden, "What We Know About Effects of Asset Holding: Implications for Research on Asset-Based Anti-Poverty Initiatives," Working Paper #96-1 (St. Louis, MO: Center for Social Development, 1996). Both of these papers may be found at <http://www.gwbssw.wustl.edu/~csd/workingpapers/workingpapers.htm.>

2. Michael Sherraden, *Assets and the Poor* (Armonk, NY: M. E. Sharpe, Inc., 1991).

3. Of course there can be competing ethical traditions that overrule the republican tradition. It is widely accepted in the United States that workers deserve some minimum level of compensation to preserve their human dignity; thus, minimum wage laws continue to have widespread support.

4. <http://cfed.cfed.org/idas/documents/whatareidas.htm>

5. Karen Edwards, "Individual Development Accounts: Creative Savings for Families and Communities," (St. Louis, MO: Center for Social Development, 1997) (see website address in note 1); *CFED IDA Handbook* (Washington, DC: Corporation for Enterprise Development, 1997) <http://cfed.cfed.org/idas/documents/idahandbook5.htm>.

6. *USAs: Universal Savings Accounts—A Route to National Economic Growth and Family Economic Security* (Washington, DC: Corporation for Enterprise Development, 1996). In *Assets for the Poor,* Sherraden used the IDA label to cover both savings accounts for the poor with cocontributions and savings accounts for the nonpoor based

on tax benefits alone. After the publication of his book IDAs came to refer specifically to the programs for the poor, and Sherraden coined the USA label for the more inclusive concept.

7. Under the Personal Responsibility and Work Opportunity Reconciliation Act of 1996, deposits by the holder of an IDA must be from earned income and cannot come out of welfare income. But if unemployed welfare recipients were allowed to make deposits from welfare income, the connection with the value of working could be maintained by giving them work to do in the IDA support agency as a form of "sweat equity" in return for cocontributions.

8. Sondra Beverly, "How Can the Poor Save? Theory and Evidence on Saving in Low-Income Households," Working Paper #97-3 (St. Louis, MO: Center for Social Development, 1997) (see website address in note 1).

9. Sherraden, *Assets and the Poor*, 267–273.

10. See ch. 5, section 4, "Assets for the Poor." For the fiscal year 2000 less money was appropriated for the demonstration program than was authorized.

11. Sherraden, *Assets and the Poor*, 227–231. Sherraden relies on the argument that tax breaks ("tax expenditures") for the better-off are the equivalent of public spending on their behalf, and therefore reducing those tax breaks is reducing welfare spending for the better-off rather than taking more of their money. While from a budgetary point of view this argument has merit, it sidesteps the political issue.

12. At the date of this writing no legislation has been introduced, and the details of the President's plan are still sketchy and subject to revision. The little information so far released by the White House is available through several sources; e.g. *New York Times*, 15 April 1999, A28.

13. See ch. 5, "Capital Assets and the Poor."

14. The success of leveraged ESOPs has been obscured by fact that the greatest growth in ESOPs has been in tax credit forms such as TRASOPs (see ch. 5, section 3). TRASOPs cost the U.S. treasury many times as much as the leveraged forms (in 1975 alone over seventy times as much, from 1977 to 1983 about eight times as much) and produce relatively little equity ownership per dollar of federal expense. Tax credit ESOPs have been estimated to produce approximately $1.25 equity ownership per dollar, while leveraged ESOPs produce approximately $2.56–$16.99 per dollar. Joseph Raphael Blasi, *Employee Ownership: Revolution or Ripoff?* (Cambridge: Ballinger Publishing Co., 1988), 80–86, 104.

15. A careful (but uncritical) delineation of Kelso's principal concepts may be found in Robert Ashford, "Louis Kelso's Binary Economy," *Journal of Socio-Economics*, 25 (1996): 1–53. Ashford's presentation is followed by a brief critique by Timothy P. Roth, "A Supply-Sider's (Sympathetic) View of Binary Economics," Ibid.: 55–68, which is a rare published critique of Kelso's ideas by a professional economist. A fuller presentation of Kelso's ideas may be found in Robert Ashford and Rodney Shakespeare, *Binary Economics: The New Paradigm* (Lanham, MD: Univ. Press of America, 1999).

16. For example, one common argument is that empirical evidence does not show the share of national income going to capital displacing the share going to labor; see Roth,

"Supply-Sider's (Sympathetic) View," 58, 61. This ignores Kelso's several objections to regarding contemporary market conditions as free enough to accurately reflect relative "productiveness"; see Louis O. Kelso and Mortimer J. Adler, *The Capitalist Manifesto* (New York: Random House, 1958), 132–134, 256–265. My point is not that Kelso's objections are necessarily sound, but that they have to be addressed. For my own critique of one aspect of Kelso's ideas, see Alan Zundel, "Kelso's Binary Economy as Social Ethics," *Journal of Socio-Economics* (forthcoming in 2000).

17. Jane Bryant Quinn, "The Virtues of Simplicity," *Newsweek*, I Feb. 1999, 33.

18. Louis O. Kelso and Patricia Hetter Kelso, *Democracy and Economic Power* (Cambridge: Ballinger Publishing Co., 1986); Stuart M. Speiser, *The USOP Handbook* (New York: The Council on International and Public Affairs, 1986); Stuart M. Speiser, ed., *Mainstream Capitalism* (New York: New Horizons Press, 1988); Stuart M. Speiser, *Ethical Economics and the Faith Community* (Bloomington, IN: Meyer-Stone Books, 1989); Stuart M. Speiser, ed., *Equitable Capitalism* (New York: The Apex Press, 1991); John H. Miller, ed., *Curing World Poverty* (St. Louis, MO: Social Justice Review, 1994); Jeff Gates, *The Ownership Solution* (Reading, MA: Addison-Wesley, 1998).

Bibliography

Appleby, Joyce. *Liberalism and Republicanism in the Historical Imagination*. Cambridge, MA: Harvard University Press, 1992.

Apter, David E., ed. *Ideology and Discontent*. New York: The Free Press of Glencoe, 1964.

Ashford, Robert. "The Binary Economics of Louis Kelso: The Promise of Universal Capitalism." *Rutgers Law Journal* 22, no. 1 (Fall 1990): 3–121.

———. "Louis Kelso's Binary Economy." *Journal of Socio-Economics* 25, no. 1 (1996): 1–53.

Ashford, Robert, and Rodney Shakespeare. *Binary Economics: The New Paradigm*. Lanham, MD: University Press of America, 1999.

Axinn, June, and Herman Levin. *Social Welfare: A History of the American Response to Need*. 3rd ed. New York and London: Longman, 1992.

Bailey, Stephen Kemp. *Congress Makes a Law: the Story Behind the Employment Act of 1946*. New York: Columbia University Press, 1950.

Banning, Lance. *The Jeffersonian Persuasion: Evolution of a Party Ideology*. Ithaca: Cornell University Press, 1978.

Bethell, Tom. "A Cruel Housing Hoax?" *American Spectator*, Feb. 1990, 11–13.

———. "Homesteading on the Liberal Plantation." *American Spectator*, April 1990, 11–12.

Beyer, Glenn H. *Housing and Society*. New York: The MacMillan Co, 1965.

Blasi, Joseph Raphael. *Employee Ownership: Revolution or Ripoff?* Cambridge, MA: Ballinger Publishing Co., 1988.

Bowler, M. Kenneth. *The Nixon Guaranteed Income Proposal: Substance and Process in Policy Change*. Cambridge, MA: Ballinger Publishing Co., 1974.

Bratt, Rachel G. *Rebuilding a Low-Income Housing Policy.* Philadelphia: Temple University Press, 1989.

Breckinridge, Sophonisba P., ed. *Public Welfare Administration in the United States: Select Documents.* 2nd ed. Chicago: University of Chicago Press, 1938.

Brock, William R. *Welfare, Democracy, and the New Deal.* Cambridge and New York: Cambridge University Press, 1988.

Brown, Josephine Chapin. *Public Relief 1929–1939.* New York: Henry Holt and Company, 1940.

Burke, Vincent J., and Vee Burke. *Nixon's Good Deed: Welfare Reform.* New York and London: Columbia University Press, 1974.

Callahan, Daniel, and Bruce Jennings, eds. *Ethics, the Social Sciences, and Policy Analysis.* New York and London: Plenum Press, 1983.

Cammisa, Anne Marie. *From Rhetoric to Reform? Welfare Policy in American Politics.* Boulder, CO: Westview Press, 1998.

Campbell, Alex. "Republicanism's New Frontier." *New Republic,* Nov. 11 1967, 15–17.

Chandler, Mittie Olion. *Urban Homesteading: Programs and Policies.* New York and Westport, CT: Greenwood Press, 1988.

Cobb, Roger W., and Charles D. Elder. *Participation in American Politics: the Dynamics of Agenda-Building.* Boston: Allyn and Bacon, Inc., 1972.

———. "Symbolic Identifications and Political Behavior." *American Politics Quarterly* 4 (July1976): 305–332.

Cohn, Jan. *The Palace or the Poorhouse: The American House as a Cultural Symbol.* East Lansing, MI: Michigan State University Press, 1979.

Davies, Pearl Janet. *Real Estate in American History.* Washington, DC: Public Affairs Press, 1958.

Dery, David. *Problem Definition in Policy Analysis.* Lawrence, KA: University Press of Kansas, 1984.

DiPasquale, Denise, and Langley C. Keyes. *Building Foundations: Housing and Federal Policy.* Philadelphia: University of Pennsylvania Press, 1990.

Donovan, John C. *The Politics of Poverty.* 2nd ed. Indianapolis and New York: Pegasus, 1973.

Dreier, Peter. "Public Housing for Sale: Private Project." *New Republic,* Aug. 4 1986, 13–15.

Edelman, Murray. *The Symbolic Uses of Politics.* Urbana, Chicago and London: University of Chicago Press, 1964.

———. *Politics As Symbolic Action: Mass Arousal and Quiescence.* Chicago: Markham Publishing Company, 1971.

———. *Political Language: Words That Succeed and Policies That Fail.* New York: Academic Press, 1977.

———. *Constructing the Political Spectacle*. Chicago: University of Chicago Press, 1988.

Elder, Charles D., and Roger W. Cobb. *The Political Uses of Symbols*. New York: Longman, 1983.

Fischer, Frank. *Evaluating Public Policy*. Chicago: Nelson-Hall Publishers, 1995.

Fischer, Frank and John Forester, ed. *The Argumentative Turn in Policy Analysis and Planning*. Durham, NC: Duke University Press, 1993.

Fisher, Robert Moore. *20 Years of Public Housing: Economic Aspects of the Federal Program*. New York: Harper and Brothers Publishers, 1959.

Foner, Eric. *Free Soil, Free Labor, Free Men: the Ideology of the Republican Party Before the Civil War*. New York: Oxford University Press, 1970.

Freedman, Leonard. *Public Housing: The Politics of Poverty*. New York: Holt, Rinehart and Winston, Inc., 1969.

Frisch, Robert A. *The ESOP Handbook: Practical Strategies for Achieving Corporate Financing Goals*. New York: John Wiley and Sons, Inc., 1995.

Gamson, William A., and Kathryn E. Lasch. "The Political Culture of Social Welfare Policy." In *Evaluating the Welfare State: Social and Political Perspectives*. Edited by Shimon E. Spiro and Ephraim Yuchtman-Yaar, ch. 22. New York and London: Academic Press, 1983.

Gamson, William A., and Andre Modigliani. "The Changing Culture of Affirmative Action." In *Research in Political Sociology*. Edited by Richard D. Braungart, v. 3: 137–177. Greenwich, CT: JAI Press, 1987.

Gates, Jeff. *The Ownership Solution: Towards a Shared Capitalism for the 21st Century*. Readings, MA: Addison-Wesley, 1998.

Ghirardo, Diane. *Building New Communities: New Deal America and Fascist Italy*. Princeton: Princeton University Press, 1989.

Graber, Doris. "Political Languages." In *Handbook of Political Communication*. Edited by Dan Nimmo and K. R. Sanders, ch. 7. Beverly Hills, CA: Sage, 1981.

Gunnell, John G. *The Descent of Political Theory: The Genealogy of an American Vocation*. Chicago: University of Chicago Press, 1993.

Hamilton, Malcolm B. "The Elements of the Concept of Ideology." *Political Studies* 35 (March 1987): 18–38.

Handler, Joel F., and Yeheskel Hasenfeld. *The Moral Construction of Poverty: Welfare Reform in America*. Newbury Park, NJ: Sage Publications, 1991.

Hawkesworth, M. E. *Theoretical Issues in Policy Analysis*. Albany: State University of New York Press, 1988.

Katz, Michael B. *Poverty and Policy in American History*. New York: Academic Press, 1983.

Katz, Michael B. *In the Shadow of the Poorhouse: A Social History of Welfare in America*. New York: Basic Books, Inc., Publishers, 1986.

Keith, Nathaniel S. *Politics and the Housing Crisis Since 1930*. New York: Universe Books, 1973.

Kelso, Louis O. "Karl Marx: The Almost Capitalist." *American Bar Association Journal* 43 (March 1957).

Kelso, Louis O., and Mortimer J. Adler. *The Capitalist Manifesto*. New York: Random House, 1958.

———. 1961. *The New Capitalists: A Proposal To Free Economic Growth From the Slavery of Savings*. New York: Random House, 1961.

Kelso, Louis O., and Patricia Hetter. *Two-Factor Theory: The Economics of Reality*. NewYork: Vintage Books, 1967.

Kelso, Louis O., and Patricia Hetter Kelso. *Democracy and Economic Power: Extending the ESOP Revolution*. Cambridge, MA: Ballinger Publishing Co., 1986.

Kingdon, John W. *Agendas, Alternatives, and Public Policies*. 2nd ed. Boston: Little, Brown & Co., 1995.

———. "Politicians, Self-Interest, and Ideas." In *Reconsidering the Democratic Public*. Edited by George E. Marcus and Russell L. Hanson, ch. 3. University Park: The Pennsylvania State University Press, 1993.

Kulikoff, Allan. *The Agrarian Origins of American Capitalism*. Charlottesville, VA and London: University Press of Virginia, 1992.

Lasswell, Harold D., and Abraham Kaplan. *Power and Society: A Framework for Political Inquiry*. New Haven: Yale University Press, 1950.

Layton, Stanford J. *To No Privileged Class: The Rationalization of Homesteading and Rural Life in the Early Twentieth-Century American West*. Salt Lake City: Charles Redd Center for Western Studies, Brigham Young University, 1988.

Leiby, James. *A History of Social Welfare and Social Work in the United States*. New York: Columbia University Press, 1978.

Levitan, Sar A. *The Great Society's Poor Law: A New Approach to Poverty*. Baltimore, MD: the John Hopkins Press, 1969.

Lichtheim, George. *The Concept of Ideology and Other Essays*. New York: Random House, 1967.

Lubove, Roy. *The Struggle for Social Security 1900–1935*. 2nd ed. Pittsburgh: University of Pittsburgh Press, 1986.

Lynn, Laurence E., Jr., and David deF. Whitman. *The President as Policymaker: Jimmy Carter and Welfare Reform*. Philadelphia: Temple University Press, 1981.

MacIntyre, Alasdair. "Utilitarianism and Cost-Benefit Analysis in Policy Making: An Essay on the Relevance of Moral Philosophy to Bureaucratic Theory." In *Ethical Theory and Business*. Edited by Tom Beauchamp and Norman Bowie. Englewood Cliffs, NJ: Prentice-Hall, Inc., 1979.

MacIntyre, Alasdair. *Whose Justice? Which Rationality?* London: Duckworth, 1988.

MacIntyre, Alasdair. *Three Rival Versions of Moral Inquiry: Encyclopaedia, Genealogy, and Tradition*. London: Duckworth, 1990.

Mannheim, Karl. *Ideology and Utopia*. London: Routledge and Kegan Paul, 1936.

Mansbridge, Jane J., ed. *Beyond Self-Interest*. Chicago: University of Chicago Press, 1990.

McClaughry, John, ed. *Expanded Ownership*. Fond Du Lac, WI: Sabre Foundation, 1972.

McClosky, Herbert. "Consensus and Ideology In American Politics." *American Political Science Review* 58 (June 1964): 361–382.

McCoy, Drew R. *The Elusive Republic: Political Economy in Jeffersonian America*. Chapel Hill, NC: University of North Carolina Press, 1980.

McLellan, David. *Ideology*. Milton Keynes, England: Open University Press, 1986.

Mead, Lawrence. *Beyond Entitlement: The Social Obligations of Citizenship*. New York: The Free Press, 1986.

———. *The New Politics of Poverty: The Nonworking Poor in America*. New York: Basic Books, 1992.

Mertz, Paul E. *New Deal Policy and Southern Rural Poverty*. Baton Rouge, LA: Louisiana State University Press, 1978.

Meyers, Marvin. *The Jacksonian Persuasion: Politics and Belief.* 2nd ed. Stanford, CA: Stanford University Press, 1960.

Miller, John H., ed. *Curing World Poverty: The New Role of Property*. Saint Louis, MO: Social Justice Review, 1994.

Mitchell, J. Paul, ed. *Federal Housing Policy and Programs: Past and Present*. New Jersey: Center for Urban Policy Research, Rutgers University, 1985.

Moynihan, Daniel P. *The Politics of a Guaranteed Income: The Nixon Administration and the Family Assistance Plan*. New York: Random House, 1973.

Murray, Charles. *Losing Ground: American Social Policy, 1950–80*. New York: Basic Books, 1984.

Patterson, James T. *America's Struggle Against Poverty 1900–1985*. 2nd ed. Cambridge, MA: Harvard University Press, 1986.

Peterson, Merrill D., ed. *Democracy, Liberty, and Property: The State Constitutional Conventions of the 1820's*. Indianapolis, New York, and Kansas City: The Bobbs-Merrill Company, Inc., 1966.

Quarrey, Michael, Joseph Blasi and Corey Rosen. *Taking Stock: Employee Ownership at Work*. Cambridge: Ballinger Publishing Company,1986.

Rachels, James. "Can Ethics Provide Answers?" *Hastings Center Report* (June 1980): 32–40.

Rein, Martin. "Value-critical policy analysis." In *Ethics, the Social Sciences, and Policy Analysis*. Edited by Daniel Callahan and Bruce Jennings, ch. 5. New York: Plenum Press, 1983.

———. *From Policy to Practice*. Armonk, New York: M. E. Sharpe, Inc., 1983.

Rejai, Mostafa. "Ideology." In *Dictionary of the History of Ideas*. Edited by Philip P. Wiener, 552–559. New York: Charles Scribner's Sons, 1973.

Ridgeway, James. "Rebuilding the Slums." *New Republic*, Jan. 7 1967, 22–25.

Rimlinger, Gaston V. *Welfare Policy and Industrialization in Europe, America, and Russia*. NewYork: John Wiley and Sons, Inc., 1971.

Rochefort, David A., and Roger W. Cobb, eds. *The Politics of Problem Definition: Shaping the Policy Agenda.* Lawrence, KA: University Press of Kansas, 1994.

Rogers, Daniel T. "Republicanism: the Career of a Concept." *The Journal of American History* (June 1992): 11–38.

Rohe, William M., and Michael Stegman. *Public Housing Homeownership Demonstration Assessment.* Chapel Hill, NC: University of North Carolina, 1990.

Roosevelt, Franklin D. "Back to the land." *Review of Reviews* 84 (Oct. 1931): 64–65.

Rosen, Corey M., Katherine J. Klein and Karen M. Young. *Employee Ownership in America: The Equity Solution.* Lexington, MA: Lexington Books, 1986.

Roth, Timothy P. "A Supply-Sider's (Sympathetic) View of Binary Economics." *Journal of Socio-Economics* 25, no.1 (1996): 55–68.

Rothman, David J. *The Discovery of the Asylum: Social Order and Disorder in the New Republic.* 2nd ed. Boston: Little, Brown and Co., 1990.

Sabatier, Paul A. "An Advocacy Coalition Framework of Policy Change and the Role of Policy-oriented Learning Therein." *Policy Sciences* 21 (1988): 129–168.

Sabatier, Paul A., and Susan Hunter. "The Incorporation of Causal Perceptions into Models of Elite Belief Systems." *Western Political Quarterly* 42 (Sep. 1989): 229–261.

Sabatier, Paul A., and Hank C. Jenkins-Smith, eds. *Policy Change and Learning: An Advocacy Coalition Approach.* Boulder, CO: Westview Press, 1993.

Salins, Peter D., ed. *Housing America's Poor.* Chapel Hill and London: University of North Carolina Press, 1987.

Schön, Donald A., and Martin Rein. *Frame Reflection: Toward the Resolution of Intractable Policy Controversies.* New York: BasicBooks., 1994

Schwartz, David C., Richard C. Ferlauto, and Daniel N. Hoffman. *A New Public Housing Policy for America: Recapturing the American Dream.* Philadelphia: Temple University Press, 1988.

Scott, William B. *In Pursuit of Happiness: American Conceptions of Property from the Seventeenth to the Twentieth Century.* Bloomington and London: Indiana University Press, 1977.

Sherraden, Michael. "Rethinking Social Welfare: Towards Assets." *Social Policy* 18, no. 3 (1988): 37–43.

———. "Stakeholding: Notes on a Theory of Welfare Based on Assets." *Social Services Review* 64, no. 4 (1990): 580–601.

———. *Assets and the Poor: A New American Welfare Policy.* Armonk NY: M. E. Sharpe, Inc., 1991.

Skocpol, Theda. *Protecting Soldiers and Mothers: The Political Origins of Social Policy in the United States.* Cambridge: The Belknap Press, 1992.

Speiser, Stuart M. *A Piece of the Action.* New York: Van Nostrand Reinhold Co., 1977.

———. *The USOP Handbook: A Guide to Designing Universal Share Ownership Plans For the United States and Great Britain.* New York: The Council on International and Public Affairs, 1986.

———, ed. *Mainstream Capitalism: Essays on Broadening Share Ownership in America and Britain*. New York: New Horizons Press, 1988.

———. *Ethical Economics and the Faith Community: How We Can Have Work and Ownership for All*. Bloomington, IN: Meyer-Stone Books, 1989.

———, ed. *Equitable Capitalism: Promoting Economic Opportunity Through Broader Capital Ownership*. New York: Apex Press, 1991.

Steiner, Gilbert Y. *Social Insecurity: The Politics of Welfare*. Chicago: Rand McNally and Co., 1966.

———. *The State of Welfare*. Washington, DC: the Brookings Institution, 1971.

Stone, Deborah A. *Policy Paradox and Political Reason*. New York: HarperCollins, 1988.

Sundquist, James L. *Politics and Policy: The Eisenhower, Kennedy, and Johnson Years*. Washington, DC: the Brookings Institution, 1968.

Torgenson, Douglas. "Between Knowledge and Politics: Three Faces of Policy Analysis." *Policy Sciences* 19 (1986): 33–59.

Trattner, Walter I. *From Poor Law to Welfare State: A History of Social Welfare in America*. 3rd ed. New York: The Free Press, 1984.

U.S. Commission on Civil Rights. *Homeownership for Lower-Income Families*. Washington, DC: U.S. Government Printing Office, 1971.

U.S. Congress, Joint Economic Committee, 94th Congress 2nd Session. *Broadening the Ownership of New Capital: ESOP's and Other Alternatives*. Washington, DC: U.S. Government Printing Office, June 17, 1976.

Weicher, John C. *Housing: Federal Policies and Programs*. Washington, DC: American Enterprise Institute for Public Policy Research, 1980.

Weir, Margaret, A. S. Orloff, and Theda Skocpol, eds. *The Politics of Social Policy in the United States*. Princeton, NJ: Princeton University Press, 1988.

Witte, Edwin E. *The Development of the Social Security Act*. Madison, WI: University of Wisconsin Press, 1962.

Wolff, Edward N. *Top Heavy: A Study of the Increasing Inequality of Wealth in America*. New York: Twentieth Century Fund Press, 1995.

Wood, Gordon S. *The Radicalism of the American Revolution*. New York: Alfred A. Knopf, 1992.

Young, Mary E. "Congress Looks West: Liberal Ideology and Public Land Policy in the Nineteenth Century." In *The Frontier in American Development*. Edited by David M. Ellis, 74–112. Ithaca. Cornell University Press, 1969.

Zundel, Alan. "Kelso's Binary Economy as Social Ethics." *Journal of Socio-Economics* (forthcoming in 2000).

Index